ALIENS AND MAN?

ALIENS AND MAN?

A SYNOPSIS OF FACTS AND BELIEFS

Jerry Kroth

Algora Publishing
New York

Library of Congress Cataloging-in-Publication Data —

Kroth, Jerome A.
    Aliens and man? A synopsis of facts and beliefs / Jerry Kroth.
      p. cm.
    Includes bibliographical references and index.
      ISBN 0-87586-816-9 (soft cover: alk. paper) — ISBN 0-87586-817-7 (hard
cover: alk. paper) — ISBN 0-87586-818-5 (ebook: alk. paper) 1. Human-alien
encounters. 2. Extraterrestrial anthropology. 3. Life on other planets. 4. Myth.
I. Title.
      BF2050.K76 2011
      001.942—dc22

                         2010035298

Printed in the United States

Endorsements

Aliens and Man is the most intellectually exciting, page-turning voyage of discovery I have been on for a very long time.
— Jeff Kisling, Ph.D., Palo Alto

... Thoroughly empirical, deeply creative, and a fascinating read!
—Marvin Forrest, Ph.D., psychotherapist, Santa Barbara,

I am enthralled! This is a refreshing leap from the encrusted time-worn answers we were all raised to believe. I have no doubt this book will be greeted as a significant contribution.
—William Yabroff, Ph.D., Professor Emeritus, Pacifica Graduate School, Author of The Inner Image

A well written, erudite book, easily available to the average reader, with or without a scientific background.
—Robert McFarland, M.D., Director of the Institute for Psychohistory: Boulder, Colorado

Jerry Kroth has pulled off an intellectual coup d'etat... This work makes me feel like we have broken "the surly bonds of earth."
—Walter Moretz, Ph.D, Professor Emeritus, George Mason University

Somewhere, something incredible is waiting to be known.
—Carl Sagan

TABLE OF CONTENTS

Table of Contents

1. Introduction to Our Journey

> *Behold the turtle. He makes progress*
> *only when he sticks his neck out.*
> —James B. Conant

I'm a psychology professor. Most of the books I've published were in subjects limited to my expertise. But having spent a few hours on the psychodynamics of myth, metaphor, and dream, I found myself sniffing around an idea that seems completely beyond the perimeters of psychology: the hypothesis that humankind had, or continues to have, some connection to extraterrestrial sources.

Before you raise your eyebrows and consider this guy just another psych prof gone berserk, let me tell you how the idea germinated.

The Psychological Bias

It begins with metaphor. Imagine a third grade boy wakes up screaming from a nightmare that *Tyrannosaurus Rex* was chasing him and about to snip off his legs. His mother tells him that *T. Rex* is extinct, hasn't been around for millions of years, and there's nothing to fear.

Well, mommy made a psychological mistake. She assumed the nightmare was "literal." She approached her son's dream as a fundamentalist religious person would: as if it were literally true. Her explanations are not likely to make a whit of difference in her little boy's life.

If clinical experience has taught us anything, it is that the dream is frequently a metaphor, a symbol pointing to something. Ask the child what's scaring him and why he's afraid. With a little empathy—and perhaps some counseling skill—mommy could learn that two sixth-grade bullies have been picking on her son, taking away his lunch money, and saying "if you tell on us, we'll bash your jaw in." He's scared to death every day he goes to school, and his nightmare is simply a metaphoric expression of a *very real situation*.

To dismiss the dream as baseless because *T. Rex* is extinct utterly misses the point.

If we look at the character of a dream, we invariably see it is a prismatic reflection of one's life told in displaced and indirect symbolism.[1] The unconscious has a curious kinship with metaphors which capture the meaning of what is transpiring in our daytime life. The frazzled third grader is not *literally* being attacked by dinosaurs, just bullies, but his protean unconscious selects a dinosaur, dragon, shark, or Rottweiler *metaphor* as the best way to portray this schoolyard conflict.

At Santa Clara University I taught clinical dream theory and interpretation at the graduate level for over fifteen years, so, if you are with me so far, let's take the next step.

Joseph Campbell, the mythologist, said we should look at myths much the way we look at dreams. "The myth is a public dream and the dream a private myth."[2] And it should be interpreted similarly. Myths are not "delusions," but they refer to something.

Take religious myths as an example. There are some 6.6 billion persons on Earth, and their religious affiliations are broken down as follows:

---

1 A comment by Joseph Griffin in *The Origin of Dreams: How and Why We Evolved to Dream* (1997) The Therapist Ltd., Halisham [page 21] reinforces this view:" That dreams use metaphor has been noted by many theorists but that all dreams use metaphor is a new finding. My research indicates that, not only do all dreams use metaphor, but that the entire dream sequence is a metaphorical expression of a waking concern."

2 http://www.mythsdreamssymbols.com/mythanddreams.html

Religion	Percent of Planet	Adherents
Christians	33%	2.01 billion
Muslims	20%	1.21 billion
No religion	15%	0.9 billion
Hinduism	13%	0.7 billion
Buddhist	6%	0.3 billion
Atheists	4%	0.2 billion
Chinese folk religions	4%	0.2 billion
New Asian religions	2%	0.2 billion
Other: Judaism, Sikh, Confucian, Baha'i, Jainism	2%	0.2 billion

Source: Information Please Almanac

If we regard all these religions as mythological systems, roughly 76 percent profess some belief in an afterlife or movement of the soul to another plane of existence after death, that is, *to another world.*

The Mouth of Hell

In other words, 76 percent of planet Earth joins in a shared mythol-ogy that espouses the transcendence of the soul into another plane of existence after death, whether passing into purgatory and then heaven (for Catholics), a metamorphosis of the soul through reincarnation (for Buddhists), an afterlife in heaven with God (for Islam), or even to eter-nal suffering in Hell (for Muslims), Christians, Hindus, Jews, in varying degrees, and, of course, Jerry Falwell). [3] [4]

Others, like Richard Dawkins who wrote *The God Delusion*, believe humanity is infected with a form of collective insanity and would assert 76 percent of the human race believes in an unrealistic set of magical ideas that only proves our species is mentally unstable. In other words, religion is "nothing-more-than" delusion.

But, in a way, that is somewhat like publishing a book for children who have nightmares called *The T. Rex Delusion* which teaches them that dinosaurs don't exist, are long gone and extinct, and fearing them is plain old silly.

Just as that little boy's nightmare-demon *points to something real*, is it not possible that our ubiquitous religious mythologies also point to something that goes beyond superstition, delusion, and irrationality?

God as Metaphor

Recent research has shown that while some myths may be pre-scientific nonsense, others function as mnemonics or symbolic ways of preserving archaic collective memory. Without written language, one means of passing on critical shared experience is through the oral tradi-tions of myth, and there are a few persuasive examples. Consider this tale of the Klamath Indians in Oregon:

> In *Visions and Memories of Paradise* . . . Richard Heinberg recounts a myth of the Klamath Indians of the Pacific Northwest in which a gigantic bird battles a monumental turtle. So far this sounds like the kind of superstitious fairy-tale supposed to have been in-

---

3 About 76% of Americans believe there is a heaven as well. Source: *Newsweek*, "Why we need heaven," August 12, 2002.

4 In parallel with these findings, a recent very large sampling of 100,000 American college students reveals 78.5% believe in God. Justin Pope, "Spiritual quest on campus." Associated Press, April 16, 2005.

vented by primitive people who explained everything by fantasy .
. . When the turtle lost the battle, Mount Mazama, the site where
he had taken his last stand, collapsed. His blood pooled into a
lake and his back protruded from the waters, forming an island.
This mythological place, the Klamath Indians say, is Crater Lake,
a magnificent site in the Cascade Mountains of Oregon. The lake,
six miles wide and 2000 feet deep, sits at over 6,000 feet above
sea level. It is known to have been formed by volcanic action that
has left the crest of the erupting mountain as an island in the lake.
In other words, Heinberg says, "the Klamath Indians . . . "have
mythologized a volcanic eruption *that actually happened* more than
6,500 years ago."

Heinberg goes on to say that myths of Aborigines in Australia also
remember prehistoric animals that have been extinct for 10–15,000
years. [5]

A far more interesting myth-
as-archaic memory is Noah's
Ark. Perhaps you see it as a
moral tale, or a divinely in-
spired story, but it also could
be a collective memory trace.

The flood myth is not limited to the Bible. It is a legend
that is found in Aztec mythology, in Central American tradition among
the Mechoacanesecs, in the epic of Gilgamesh fifteen centuries before
Noah's Ark was transcribed in the Old Testament, and in Indian tribes
of Ecuador.

As the flood myth repeats, so too does the figure of Noah.

More than 500 deluge legends are known around the world, and,
in a survey of 86 of these (20 Asiatic, 3 European, 7 African, 46
American and 10 from Australia and the Pacific . . . researcher Dr.
Richard Andree concluded that 62 *were entirely independent* of the
Mesopotamian and Hebrew accounts.[6]

---

5 Myth in Metahistory Part One The Panorama of the Past Source= http://www.
meta history.org/MythMetahistory1.asp See also: Richard Heinberg, *Memories
and Visions of Paradise.* IL: Quest Books, Dec. 1994,
6 Hancock, Ibid., p. 193.

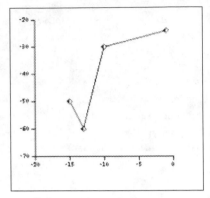

Temperature of Greenland Ice Sheets for the Last 15,000 Years

If 62 independently aris-ing tales all have a very similar deep structure, the myth could be interpreted *as referring to a real event.* In fact it has been sug-gested that the ubiquity of this story may point to the retreat of the massive ice sheets that covered the planet.

From 11,000 BC until 9,000 BC, a mile-thick ice cap receded. Ice age mammals were found as far south as Texas. The graphic of the tem-perature of the Greenland ice sheet shows a rapid rise in temperature in about 11,000 BC. Thousands of animal species became extinct, and the oceans rose 350 feet. Deglaciation-induced flooding may be a realistic explanation for all the consequent flood myths.[7]

So, is it not possible that the universality of the flood myth can be understood as a human archaic memory of a natural threat to man's survival?

Just as Noah's Ark might serve as a memory trace of a real event like deglaciation and flooding, and aboriginal myths could be ways of remembering long-extinct animals that inhabited that landscape, per-haps the human preoccupation with God or the Gods similarly could be an archaic memory—preserved, repeated, and recapitulated—as an awkward 'as if' attempt to remember that our ancestors were once vis-ited by other beings.

That is how this hypothesis got started: *T. Rex* as a symbolic refer-ent for very real bullies. *Gods* as symbolic referents for very real extra-terrestrial encounters.

---

7 Source for the graph on temperature over Greenland R.B. Alley "The Two-Mile Time Machine," 200

Still sound crazy? Well, if so, come with me on a short side trip to the Caroline Islands.

John Frum: Reality to Myth and Back Again

In asking whether the *Homo sapiens* sense of his Gods was, or could be, an archaic memory of contact with extraterrestrials the "cargo cult" of the Caroline Islands and the cult of John Frum is an astonishing paradigm for how humanity *might have reacted* to an extraterrestrial visit. On its face, this seems an extremely attractive psychological explanation for the very origin of religious beliefs.

John Frum allegedly was an American who flew his small, single engine plane landing in the primitive and isolated Ellis Islands in the South Pacific in World War II. He was carrying "cargo." The peoples on these islands had never seen an airplane, and encountered for the first time in their lives this incredible new technology. His "heavenly" arrival gathered about itself all the dimensions necessary to become a supernatural event.

> They tried to attract the flying gods by creating 'airfields' of their own and populating them with bamboo 'airplanes' and 'refrigerators' then moving around them in ritual dances meant to emulate the airman. Some cargo cultists . . . even worshipped the back cover of an old Agatha Christie paperback they found on the ground.[8]

The pilot was deified and natives memorialized these events, awaiting more cargo and the second coming of their God, John Frum.

> When he comes we will have riches," he said. "We will have lorries, iceboxes, and concrete houses. We will have education. We will be free."
> The cult is exclusive to Tanna, one of the southernmost islands in the South Pacific nation. Accounts of John Frum's origins are as copious as they are colorful, but it is broadly agreed that he first appeared in human form in the late 1930s or early 1940s.

---

8 Whitley Stieber, Ibid., p. 88.

Costumed John Frum dancer on John Frum Day.

The movement snowballed after the Second World War . . . They decided that John Frum was American — perhaps John "frum" America. To encourage his return, they engaged in rituals, and twice-daily hoist the American and US navy flags. On Feb 15 — John Frum Day — men stage military-style marches, with "USA" emblazoned on their backs and spears slung over their shoulders to represent rifles.[9]

At first glance this seems embarrassingly primitive, but it is a psychologically *reasonable* reaction of a naive people to an encounter with a being that possessed awesome technology, resources, and superiority never before encountered.

If this earth was visited by extraterrestrials in its early history, then a plausible psychological reaction to such an event, or events, would be to deify these entities exactly as the John Frum cultists have done. In the course of time, it is even possible to imagine how local religious superstitious could wrap the memory in hyperbole and spread the myths forward until full blown religions appear where we arrive at a single, omniscient, omnipresent, and omnipotent Godhead who promises a second coming accoutered with a divine cargo of goodies and salvation.

The roots of *Homo sapiens* religious fixations indeed may reside in something as shamefully simple as this John Frum template.

We might draw from this story a mild sense that the prolific and ubiquitous stories of creatures descending from the heavens and then ascending once again might be less fictitious and hallucinatory than we

---

9 Source: http://www.religionnewsblog.com/7166-John_Frum_is_given_his_marching_orders.html

would otherwise think. They could be John-Frum-like *memorializations in myth.*

Instead of thinking of them as delusions, fables, and fairy-tales, could they possibly describe real events? If we hold to the politically correct view that myths are delusions with no referent in reality, we should pause to remember the story of Troy described in the *Iliad.* The account was also deemed a fantasy until Heinrich Schliemann set out to see if Troy were a real place. With a little digging, he proved the myth was an accurate record and a bona fide memory.

Sir Arthur Evans, fascinated by Theseus killing the Minotaur, and disbelieving his contemporaries who said such stories were mere loquacious fantasy, unearthed Knossos and the Minoan civilization of Crete.

This story of discovery repeats many times over as archeologists uncovered Nineveh, the city of Ur, Babylon, Sumer, Acadia, the ancient birthplace of Abraham, the kingdom of King Sargon II, even Babel . . . all thought to be the stuff of fables, legends, and allegories instead of concrete collective recollections of real places stored in the archives of mythology.

Sir Arthur Evans, British archeologist

One hundred and fifty years ago, much of the history in the Old Testament was considered pure fiction, including the existence of Sumeria (the biblical Shinar), Akkad, and Assyria. But those forgotten pieces of our past were discovered in the late nineteenth and early twentieth centuries when Nineveh and Ur were found."[10]

... "Myths" of the Bible that referred to a number of legendary ancient cities and peoples were slowly proved to be *factual history*.[11]

Indeed myths have proven to be a mother lode of scientific discovery.[12]

So, if we follow this reasoning out, what if mankind's ubiquitous fascination with his Gods and rituals directed toward the heavens was *more than* just an expression of a human need to think someone up there cared?

Just as the Deluge myth may memorialize the recession of the ice age—a real event which otherwise would succumb to the Neolithic fog of human forgetfulness—could our vast supply of God-myths represent memory traces of encounters with extraterrestrials?

Certainly we have all had our dose of ET lore, and from the outset we know that much of this "evidence" is popularized just for fun and it is too "far out" for most of us to give any credit. Secondly, this text is not selling or proselytizing New Age esoterica about ET communicating, watching, or interacting with mankind. This is not a rationalization for pseudo-scientific speculation or sensationalism. Yes, this book is hypothetical, but it is not *Geraldo*.

What we intend to do between these pages is to sort and sift through reams of data and expunge the kooky, tacky, sensational, and bizarre, and then ask if anything remains which is suggestive of extraterrestrial visitations . . . any data, in other words, satisfying a higher standard of evidence than what that sensationalist books and on tabloid TV.

Our next few chapters chapter then will explore the hypothesis that the Gods represents some kind of primitive memory trace *Homo sapiens* had of an extraterrestrial encounter or encounters which his mythologies have encoded, encrypted, and memorialized over the ages.

10 Will Hart, Ancient Agriculture, in search of the missing links, in *Forbidden History*, *ibid.*, p. 195.

11 Will Hart, *Ibid.*, p. 71.

12 In 2008, the ancient city of the Khazars, similarly thought to be only a fable, was found in Russia. Source: http://news.yahoo.com/s/ap/20080920/ap_on_re_eu/russia_lost_capital

When I admitted to myself that this idea was worth at least a cursory look, I had no idea I would walk into such a vast and exciting aggregation of evidence.

In beginning the journey, there are four areas to explore: archeology, mythology, the literature of the paranormal, and the mercurial field of evolutionary biology. These four branches grow from a gargantuan tree, and as we prune out the freakish and far-fetched, if anything edible remains, hopefully we'll recognize it.

> *Why not go out on a limb?*
> *That's where the fruit is.*
> —Will Rogers

2. Archeological Intimations of Ancient Visitations

Shrines! Shrines! Surely you don't believe in the gods.
What's your argument? Where's your proof?
—Aristophanes, 411 BC

We start slowly because there are many academic controversies weighing us down when we entertain this hypothesis. First, we stumble, or trip, over Erich Von Daniken who writes of ancient astronauts riding *Chariots of the Gods.* After forty-four million copies of that book were sold, his thesis fell into serious disrepute in the academic world largely because Von Daniken is a flagrant popularizer with question-

able scholarship, references, and interpretations. Just check his footnotes sometime . . . if he provides them.

Nazca lines in Peru as seen from the air

Von Daniken, for example, holds that the unusual figures of Nazca plains in Peru, which can only be seen from the air, were landing areas for ancient spacecraft. If extraterrestrials could fly light years across interstellar space, why would they need special zones mapped out by the local primitives to aid them?

Pop Archeology

Before getting into the more serious exhibits on our virtual museum tour, consider the "Von Daniken effect" more closely. In the early stages of this movement, a number of artifacts were catapulted into popular consciousness, which seemed to have only two distinguishing qualities: (a) they were very old, and (b) they looked weird. That seemed all that was necessary to catch the burgeoning interest of archeological groupies. Here are two such examples:

A ceiling painting on a beam found in a 3,000 year old New Kingdom Temple near Cairo depicts what looks remarkably like a helicopter and some old Buck Roger's space ships.

And then there are the Dogu figurines in Japan roughly estimated to be about 2,500 years old. These ancient objects depict strange mechanical devices and what curiously looks like a space suit.

So they are very old and they look like space ships, space suits, or flying vehicles. Okay, but shouldn't our standards of evidence be a bit loftier?

Enter Zecharia Sitchin, a more scholarly version of Von Daniken and skilled in translating ancient Sumerian. His books (*Genesis Revisited, The Earth Chronicles, The 12th Planet*

) have similarly done extremely well as they echo his underlying theme that extraterrestrials visited here and called themselves the *Anunnaki*. Apparently they reside on a very, very cold planet beyond Pluto.

Actually the work of Von Daniken, Sitchin, and pop archeology has a good side. The cumulative interest generated by this movement spawned far more research. The findings unearthed by those who followed these pop pioneers are quite bewitching, and they get more interesting every year.

For example, a researcher was wandering through the Egyptian Museum of Antiquities.[1] He discovered an object previously thought to be a figurine dated to about 200 BC. It turned out to be a seven-inch wooden airplane made out of sycamore *which could actually fly.*

Egyptian sycamore glider

It possessed characteristics never found in birds, yet which are part of modern aircraft design. Dr. Messiha, a former model plane enthusiast, immediately recognized the aircraft features and persuaded the Egyptian Ministry of Culture to investigate.

Made of very light sycamore, the craft weighs 0.5 oz. with straight and aerodynamically shaped wings, spanning about 7 inches. A separate slotted piece fits onto the tail precisely like the back tail wing on a modern plane.

A full-scale version could have flown carrying heavy loads, but at low speeds, between 45 and 65 miles per hour. What is not known, however, is what the power source was. The model makes a perfect glider as it is. Even though over 2,000 years old, it will soar a considerable distance with only a slight jerk of the hand. Fully restored balsa replicas travel even farther.[2]

Ancient Egyptians, it would appear, had some knowledge of aerodynamics far earlier than believed.[3]

Chinese, Mexican & Egyptian Pyramids

Most Americans are unaware there are pyramids in China. Photos taken in 1945 by the U.S. Air Force revealed over a hundred. The area was closed off to foreigners for a considerable time and is near the site of Chinese rocket launches. The Chinese seem averse to foreign attention drawn to these structures and actually planted conifers to hide them from archeological or aerial probing.

Chinese 'White' pyramid (top) and Mexico's Pyramid of the Sun

When Egyptologists discuss Egyptian pyramids, their theories curiously do not connect into a more macroscopic view to include other similar monuments elsewhere on the planet. Few look at the whole panorama of earthly pyramids to propose a more global hypothesis.

The Chinese pyramid, for example, is estimated to be some 2200 years old and, originally, the tallest pyramid in the world at over a thousand feet. Its design is remarkably similar to the Pyramid of the Sun in Mexico also estimated to be

2,000 years old and the third tallest pyramid in the world and made from over three million tons of material.

Would it not be reasonable to suggest that similarities of these unusual structures demand a more global theory with regard to their origin? These are *strange* human constructions, and yet their appearance thousands of miles distant from one another, and separated by epochs in time, might lead one to wonder if there was some connection between them. How could the pyramids of Egypt, Mexico, and China be related to one another?

Mythology certainly offers an answer. As the Egyptians trace their origins to the stars, local Chinese lore explains the construction of its pyramids coming from the age of the "old emperors" who reigned in China. Allegedly these emperors did not originate on earth. They were the descendants of the "sons of heaven who roared down to this planet on their fiery metallic dragons."

As the Chinese reference the "sons of heaven," the Egyptians footnote their gods, Osiris and Horus, while the Aztecs bowed to Huitzilopochtli and Tlaloc . . . all deities mysteriously connected to these monuments.

The Belt of Orion

Giza pyramid plane

An American engineer working in Saudi Arabia often took his children to Egypt. Fascinated by the and a surveyor by trade, he enjoyed camping near the base of the pyramids, but found the layout of the three largest pyramids near Giza puzzling. They were built with incredibly exacting standards but laid out with respect to each other *mysteriously off-center.* He could not understand how Egyptian engineering could be so precise and yet the locations of the pyramids *skewed . . .* unless, of course, they were skewed by intention.

One evening, lying in the sand and looking up at the stars near his tent, he had a mind-boggling insight. He could see that the constellation Orion, directly above, was off center too and did not fit a straight line. He measured the displacement and orientation of stars and spent the larger part of the remainder of his life examining the analogous similarities down here on earth in the organization plan of the three pyramids. His findings were so accurate and intriguing Egyptologists agreed to publish his work even though he had few credentials beyond a civil engineering background to gain access to elite professional journals.

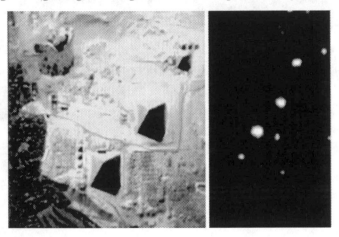

Photo of Giza pyramids appearing in this section, courtesy of the Institute of Collective Behavior and Memory

The locations of the three major pyramids in Giza are "off" by an analogous amount that the three stars in Orion *vary* from a straight line. The pyramids, he concludes, are like dropping a plumb line down from the stars, an attempt to make a heavenly city on earth.

The theory goes further.

What were thought to be airshafts within the pyramid focus themselves exactly on Sirius on two dates, each 13,000 years separated from the next. If this theory is correct, and the shafts were set to align with Sirius on these dates, then the Egyptians clearly knew about precession (the wobble effect) of the planet and that it would take roughly 13,000 years before the next alignment with Sirius was set. [Note that a line drawn through the Belt of Orion points to Sirius.] Not only is the astronomy and geometry uncanny, but also the entire purpose of the pyramids needs rethinking. Their purpose, to this author, was to launch the spirit of the pharaoh back to his stellar birthplace.

Aerial view of pyramids in Egypt (left), in China (right), and the Belt of Orion (below) left.

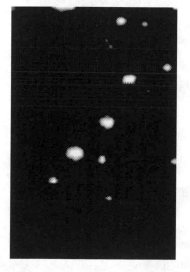

The three figures of the Egyptian pyramid plane, the Chinese pyramid plane, and the belt of Orion create an angle of roughly 15 degrees of arc.

These shafts were considered 'travel tubes' for the soul of the pharaoh to return to his heavenly origin.

What is even more curious is that the pyramid layout in Egypt is very similar to the skewness of the pyramids in China, as if both sets of structures parallel the dogleg skewness of the Belt of Orion. Now to really boggle your mind, we are required to add into these observations another curious finding. Researchers Christopher Knight and Alan Butler report in *Before the Pyramids* that they found yet another such monument, this time in Neolithic England.

A "henge" is an earthen mound-like structure or set of structures. The Thornborough henges trace out a pattern similar to the above pyramid planes in China and Egypt. Alan Butler took photos of Orion's belt, put them into a computer program, blew them up until the longest line measured 366 cm on his drawing program. He then took the Google Earth image of the Thornborough henges and drew lines as he had done with the stars in the belt of Orion.

> I drew lines as I had done with the stars and then increased the lines proportionally until the longer line. . . was 366 cm long on the drawing program. I then noted that the shorter line . . . was exactly (not nearly, not very nearly, but quite exactly) a tiny bit under 360 cm. Result. The Thornborough henges are not a good copy of Orion's Belt, they are not even a very good copy of Orion's Belt. They are an exact, absolutely, absolutely, absolutely *exact copy* of Orion's Belt.[9]

Layout of Thornborough henges, aerial view

Is it merely a coincidence that disparate cultures, each unaware of the other, built similar structures, one in Neolithic England, one in China, and another in Egypt, following almost identical plot plans, with the tiniest structure doglegging off to the left from an otherwise exact set of surveyor standards?

All of this, to believe conventional archeology, happened entirely by coincidence and without any contact between cultures. Moreover, the fact that these engineering feats are attributed to the heavens or the influence of "the Gods" is abjectly ignored in academia. Seems at the very least curious.

Another set of buildings, the Yonaguni monuments, was discovered off the shores of Okinawa. Preliminary estimates say they may be as much as 10,000 years old.[1] If we add into this whole mix of pyramids in the Canary Islands, China, Egypt, Mexico, and Guatemala, the firmness of the ground on which our present anthropology stands in asserting all these monuments were built *indigenously and independently* feels a bit mushy. Not only do these unusual structures seem to have incredible similarities, but the way they were laid out implicates an eerie connection to the stars.

Pi and Phi

We were taught that Archimedes in the third century BC discovered *pi* and calculated it correctly at 3.14. However, if one calculates the height of the Great Pyramid at Giza, which was built far earlier than Archimedes, and multiplies that by *2pi*, the exact perimeter of its base is defined, hardly a mathematical accident. Similarly, in Mexico, the height of the Pyramid of the Sun x *4pi* equals the perimeter of its base. The perimeter is 2,932.8 feet, and that calculation is *less than half an inch* from this true perimeter.

The Pyramid of the Sun in Teotihuacan, Mexico. The third largest pyramid in the world made from 30 million cubic feet of earth. The structure was then layered with stone and then coated with brilliant-colored plaster. The plaster is now gone. The pyramid encrypts pi in its construction. It was built at the time of Christ allegedly by the Teotihuacanos whose hieroglyphic language has yet to be decoded.

According to Livio Catullo Stecchini, an American professor of the History of Science and an acknowledged expert on ancient measurement, the evidence for the existence of such anomalous knowledge in antiquity is irrefutable.[1]

The Great Pyramid of Giza

> ...is essentially a scale model of Earth and a geodesic marker of the center of Earth's landmass. The ratio of the pyramid's height to its perimeter equals the ratio of Earth's radius to its circumference.[12]

Pythagoras was credited with the discovery of *Phi*, an irrational number called the Golden Section, or the Divine Proportion, but two millennia prior *Phi* is found in the construction of the King's Chamber of the Great Pyramid at Giza. It was also found in Luxor.[13]

An interesting, contemporary account of *Phi* is given in the *The Da-Vinci Code*. Here is an excerpt:

> Nobody understood better than DaVinci the divine structure of the human body. DaVinci actually exhumed corpses to measure the exact proportion of human bone structure. He was the first to show the human body is literally made of building blocks whose proportional ratios always equal *PHI*...Try it. Measure the distance from the tip of your head to the floor. Then divide that by the distance from your belly button to the floor. Guess what number you get?
>
> "Not *PHI*!" one of the jocks blurted out in disbelief.
>
> "Yes, *PHI*," Langdon replied. "One-point-six-one-eight. Want another example? Measure the distance from your shoulder to your fingertips, and then divide it by the distance from your elbow to your fingertips. *PHI* again. Another? Hip to floor divided by knee to floor. *PHI* again. Finger joints. Toes, spinal divisions. *PHI*. *PHI*. *PHI*. My friends, each of you is a walking tribute to the Divine Proportion.
>
> . . . *PHI* appeared in the organization structures of Mozart's sonatas, Beethoven's Fifth Symphony, as well as the works of Bartok, Debussy, and Schubert . . . In closing, Langdon said, walking to the chalkboard, "we return to symbols." He drew

five intersecting lines that formed a five-pointed star. "This symbol is one of the most powerful images you will see this term.
Formally known as a pentagram—or pentacle, as the ancients
called it—this symbol is considered both divine and magical by many cultures . . . because if you draw a pentagram, the
lines automatically divide themselves into segments according to the Divine Proportion . . . the ratios of line segments in a
pentacle all equal *PHI*, making this symbol the ultimate expression of the Divine Proportion. For this reason, the five-pointed
star has always been the symbol for beauty and perfection.[14] . . .

However ubiquitous and important *Phi* is, the traditional notion
that Pythagoras discovered it now seems untrue. It appears to have
been known and incorporated into one of the earliest structures made
by man, far earlier than the time of Pythagoras, and can be found in its
exactness in Giza.[15]

Another example of the precocity of our so-called primitive, backward, ancestors is the computation of the solar year. The Gregorian
calendar computed the exact length of the solar year as 365.2422 days,
incorporating an error of just 0.0003 of a day.[16] [17] That represented the
pinnacle of scientific knowledge in the sixteenth century. The Mayan
calendar, however, achieved greater accuracy far earlier than that computing the solar year with an error of only 0.0002 of a day.

We are not left merely in the hands of Von Daniken and the tabloid press. Knowledge of *pi* and *Phi* reaches far back into antiquity along
with a scrupulously and exacting astronomy and mathematics.

Indeed, at the time of its construction, the height of the Great Pyramid was said to be 147 meters, and the distance of the earth from the
sun at its closest point is 147 million kilometers.[18] Multiply the height
of the pyramid by one billion, and you get the distance of the earth to
the sun at the perihelion. The distance from the earth to the sun was
not known or calculated until 1860, yet is it possible the architects of
the Great Pyramid suffused that little tidbit of astrophysics into their
monument as well?

Maybe we can dismiss these facts as lucky coincidences, but a competing point of view is that 4,400 years ago, a civilization of incredible
brilliance existed which was one of the very *first* recorded civilizations

our species produced. And let us not forget that in its mythology, *it attributed its genius, its origin, and even its language to non-earthly sources.*

Knowledge of the Solar System?

A Sumerian clay tablet, dated at roughly 4,500 years of age, portrays the sun surrounded by nine planets.[19]

Perhaps these glyphs are making reference to an old God, his wife, and his nine concubines, but is it entirely absurd to suppose this might be an accurate description of our own nine-planet solar system rotating about the sun?

The Maps of Pyri Reis and Oronteus Finaeus

If the conjecture is true, then the heliocentric theory, originating with Copernicus five hundred years ago, was known 4,500 years earlier.[20] And the ninth planet, Neptune—not discovered until 1930—was somehow in human awareness four millennia prematurely.[21]

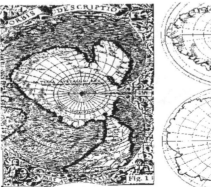
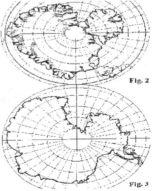

Figure 1 - *Oronteus Finaeus map of 1531, southern hemisphere*
Figure 2 - *The Oronteus Finaeus map redrawn on a modern polar projection*
Figure 3 - *A modern map of Antarctica drawn on a modern polar projection. Source: William Fuller, http://members.tripod.com/~Zomb/ANTARCTI.HTM*

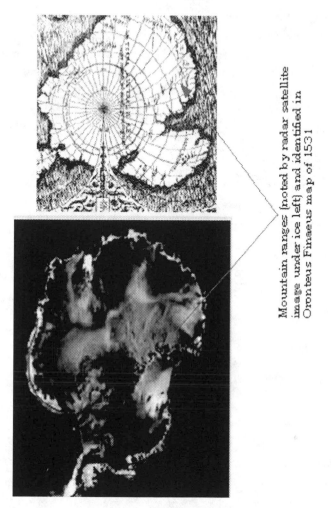

Mountain ranges (noted by radar satellite image under ice left) and identified in Oronteus Finaeus map of 1531

Curiously, in 2200 BC, Hindus and Assyrians represented Saturn with a ring of serpents, but no other planets were given rings.[22] Were these symbolic serpents again just lucky coincidences? If not, how did Hindus, two millennia before Christ, come to know Saturn had rings?

Another mystery points also in the direction that *Homo sapiens* had deep knowledge of the world much earlier than supposed. In the early 1500s a Turkish navigator, Admiral Pyri Reis, drew maps of the world which he said were *based upon earlier maps* from which he worked.

The map of Pyri Reis dates to AD 1513.

What is remarkable is that the map describes rather accurately the continent of Antarctica. More peculiarly, it depicts mountain ranges and flowing rivers which correspond to images of the continent seismically surveyed *only in 1949*. A second map, the Oronteus Finaeus Map of 1531, showed Antarctica with non-glacial conditions in Queen Maud Land, Victoria Land, and the East coast of the Ross Sea. How could that be possible?

Antarctica was discovered by Captain Cook in 1799 but so shrouded in ice, he could not map its interior. From the Oronteus Finaeus map, also copied from earlier sources, ancient mariners were able to identify a mountain range that existed on the continent and also to have outlined its features when it was covered by an ice sheet miles thick. How was that possible? Modern projection techniques when applied to the map show it possesses uncanny accuracy. According to William Fuller:

> The Oronteus Finaeus map is more accurate than any map made anywhere up to the year 1800. Not only does this map show the entire continent of Antarctica, but also inland rivers and mountain ranges. These are no fanciful creations, the river beds and mountain ranges actually exist although today they are buried by a mile-thick cap. This fact was unknown until (the International Geophysical Year) when teams scientists did sonar tests of the ice which mapped coastline beneath it. The modern maps match the old maps exactly. [23]

Professor Charles Hapgood, author of *Maps of the Ancient Sea Kings*, [24] says the only way to know that mountain ranges existed on Antarctica was to have seen or witnessed them *before* their glaciation. The earliest time when Antarctica was not entirely covered by ice was approximately 4000 BC. If someone explored Antarctica, mapped its perimeter, and identified its mountain ranges, those surveys had to be performed *prior to the fourth millennium.*[25]

The only problem with that conjecture is that there were no recorded civilizations then. Bit of a problem. Sumer and Egypt did not appear until the third millennium.[26]

Longitude, we thought, was mastered in the 1720s, but these maps seem to betray knowledge of longitude and the capacity to do spherical trigonometry, the mathematics involved in computing projections on a globe."[27]

Baalbek in Lebanon

One Russian scientist opines that,

> . . . between the 5th and 10th millennium BC, there was a civiliza-
> tion on Earth that possessed great knowledge in the field of navi
> gation, cartography, and astronomy, which was no less advanced
> than that of the 18th century.[28]

Obviously this is not exculpatory evidence proving extraterrestrials visited earth. It merely points to some lost and advanced civilizations that seem to have left traces. It is possible some kind of advanced
society existed prior to this time antedating our knowledge of our own
civilization. Skilled in mathematics, language, cartography, and astronomy, and through some unknown process of diffusion, it managed
to spread its influences to the Egyptians and the Chinese as well as to
have mapped Antarctica. Granting all that, *it still it could have been just a
human society.* A good example is mythic Atlantis. That is a reasonable
supposition. It does offer to explain away a lot of this data.

But it is also possible to proffer a competing suggestion, namely
that there could have been some extraterrestrial involvement or interaction with mankind which helped to produce these anomalies as well.

Baalbek, Peru, and Bolivia

There are 'lesser' mysteries that baffle our preconceived notions of a backward, undeveloped ancient world. Not only are the masonry and stone cutting techniques notable in the construction of the Egyptian pyramids, but one giant carved stone in the Middle East at Baalbek is 1,100 tons, seventy two feet long, and the largest piece of hewn rock on the face of the earth. That one, single, sculpted rock weighs in at 2.4 million pounds! To budge it one inch would require an army of more than 16,000 workers. The enormous crawler which is currently used by NASA to move the Saturn V rocket is the only machine on earth today which could move this monolith.

In Sacsayhuaman above Cuzco, Peru similar unwieldy megaliths were found perfectly cut, carried, and placed. Some of these blocks weigh 300,000 pounds and are

> . . . fitted together perfectly. The enormous stone blocks are cut, faced, and fitted so well that even today one cannot slip the blade of a knife, or even a piece of paper between them. No mortar is used, and no two blocks are alike . . . Each individual stone had to have been planned well in advance, a twenty ton-stone, alone one weighing 80 to 200 tons, cannot just be dropped casually into position with any hope of attaining that kind of accuracy. The stones are locked and dovetailed into position, making them earthquake-proof.

150 ton stone

Indeed, after many devastating earthquakes in the Andes over the last few hundred years, the blocks are still perfectly fitted while the Spanish Cathedral in Cuzco has been leveled twice. Even more incredibly, the blocks are not local stone, but by some reports came from quarries in Ecuador, almost 1,500 miles away. Others have located quarries a good deal closer, only five miles or so away. Though this fantastic fortress was supposedly built just a few hundred years ago by the Incas, they have no record of having built it, nor does it figure in any of their legends. How is it that the Incas who reportedly had no knowledge of higher mathematics, no written language, no iron tools, and did not even use the wheel, are credited with having built this cyclopean complex of walls and buildings? Frankly, one must literally grope for an explanation, and it is not an easy one.

Another investigator cited by Childress tried to explain the origin of the rocks from a nearby quarry to Cuzco. He made the following observation:

Sacsayhuaman, Peru. These impossibly engineered megaliths not only are a mystery of construction but the entire complex is as well. The stones are organized to cut an angle of six degrees so that when the winter solstice occurs shadows are cast to fall precisely at the foot of the protruding walls (to my left). In addition, the entire complex is an acoustic marvel with echoes focused precisely on a central point across a plaza the size of a football field.

The largest stone . . . weighs about 150 tons. It could have been pulled up a ramp with a force of about 260,000 pounds . . . such a feat would have required a minimum of some 2,400 men. Getting the men seemed possible, but where did they all stand? . . . Further perplexing . . . is that the stones of Sacsayhuaman were finely dressed, yet are not polished, showing no signs of dragging. He could not figure out how they were transported the 22 miles from the Rumiqolqa quarry.

The stones of Baalbek and Cuzco show no signs of having been dragged. How were they cut, moved, or placed? And why were such large stones used rather than cut into more manageable pieces? According to David Childress:

> If they had cut the stone into, say, 100 pieces, they would still be of unusually large size, larger than a man, but at least could have been stacked into a wall much more easily. One is left with the unsettling thought that the reason they used these huge stones was because they *could* use them—and do it relatively easily, though today we have no idea how.

Anthropologists nonchalantly talk about the Neolithic periods of hunter gatherers who still have no written language, trap fish, make beads, and are only in the early stages of domesticating plants, but right alongside of these primitive peoples, we find inscrutable megaliths and pyramids built using mathematics, astronomy, and intricate construction technologies which absolutely mystify us.

Only recently did archeologists discover a large pyramid and temple-observatory in Peru antedating by 800 years all archeological assessments of when advanced civilization took root in the Americas. The ancient observatory precisely predicts the solstices, and was built *within 400 years of Giza over 7,000 miles away.*

> "It is really quite a shock to everyone . . . to see sculptures of that sophistication coming out of a building of that time period," says Yale archeologist Richard Burger[32]
> . . . Even the name of the culture which inhabited the region remains unknown, because "writing did not emerge in the Americas for 2,000 more years."[33]

It is one thing to claim that extraterrestrials built these structures all over the globe. That is still an audacious speculation. However, to say that it is *preposterous* to suggest an advanced, superior, precipitant-yet-still-unknown culture existed is equally questionable: pyramids, hieroglyphs, hewn rocks, ancient maps, precise calendars, all with an unanticipated precocity in astronomy, navigation, and civil engineering and *not localized or confined to any one part of the earth* . . . these are anomalies which, at least, have every right to pique our curiosity.

Puma Punktu

Another monument is Puma Punktu near Lake Titicaca in Bolivia. These ruins are truly startling. Gigantic rocks of granite with precise grooves and fittings have been found scattered across the landscape. Some of them are so perfectly sculpted that they interlocked to form walls. In some fittings, a razor bland cannot fit between these joints.

The "Gate of the Sun," this structure was originally made out of one piece of solid rock; located near Puma Punktu in Tiahuanaco, courtesy of www.inkatour.com. Cut stones on right were made to fit together.

The original structure stood some 56 feet tall and stretched for a kilometer. Said to rival the structures of Easter Island, the Great Pyramid, and Stonehenge, Puma Punktu is puzzling. The entire complex is situated on a plateau at 13,000 feet where there are no trees or logs for transporting or rolling these huge megaliths. One stone alone weighs 900,000 pounds!

Traditional archeologists say that it was built by the Tiwanaku culture about 1500 BC, but skeptics suggest it could be as old as 15,000 BC.[34] What makes this area so exciting to devotes of the "ancient astronaut" point of view is perhaps best articulated by Maleeka Spriggs:

> The real mystery lies in how Puma Punktu was built. Many of the blocks weighed 200 tons, with one even weighing in at 450 tons!

How were these blocks brought to a plateau 13,000 feet high? While Stonehenge's method is often explained as stones being rolled on tree trunks, the tribe would have had no access to trees on the barren plateau. The wheel had supposedly not been invented by that point, leaving archaeologists without an explanation.[35]

Puma Punktu stone with drill holes and lines which appear "machined."

Not only did the Tiwanaku culture not have the wheel, but they did not have the tools necessary to cut granite, transport it, and, to top it off, they had no formal system of writing. According to Giorgio Tsoulakis, "compared to Puma Punktu, the pyramids are child's-play. . . The blocks were so finely cut that they perfectly interlocked." Says another commentator "there's actually evidence of machining and that they were using machine tools . . . The lines cut into these rocks are exactly straight and precisely the same depth from one end to the other . . . The tools had to be tipped with diamonds."[36]

Puma Punktu is one of our many archeological exhibits: stunning stone work, architecturally baffling, unknown as to its significance or purpose, and yet with traditional archeology predictably evangelizing these ancient structures certainly had nothing to do with extraterrestrials, were constructed by an illiterate indigenous population which made these monuments all by themselves and without contact with other indigenous peoples who were—accidentally and coincidentally—doing very similar strange things with granite and blocks of stone all over the globe in very, very, ancient times.

A Footnote about Scientific Humility and Speculation

A thoroughly enjoyable scientific read is Bill Bryson's, *A Short History of Nearly Everything.* It reminds us of how flimsy our scientific knowledge is. Take the emergence of humankind. Bryson says that fossils are extremely difficult to form and avoid degradation over time. Those few we have discovered from Australopithecus to Lucy to Neanderthal to the earliest *Homo sapiens*—that is, the rare fossilized bones and fragments from which we have reconstructed the entire history of mankind—could all fit in the back of a pick-up truck. In other words, all the raw empirical evidence used to reconstruct our five million year journey from chimps through all the hominid variants to our present species can fit in the back of a Chevy. Kind of makes you a bit cautious in attaching high levels of confidence to present scientific formulations about mankind's evolution and origins.

Suggesting that Puma Punktu may be 17,000 years old obviously contradicts mainstream archeology, which says that migrations occurred into the Americas only about 11,000 years ago. [37] Oops, a few years after that pronouncement, an archeologist reported that fossilized human excrement found in Oregon carbon dated to 14,300 years. [38]

Well, okay, then, 14,300 years ago there were migrations across the Bering Strait, but not 17,000 years ago! But, oops again, a 2009 study analyzed the dispersion of genes in the Americas and pushed back the date to 17,000 years. [39]

Then, to top it off, Professor Silvia Gonzalez of John Moore's University discovered a human footprint in volcanic ash in central Mexico carbon dated to 40,000 years. [40]

All of this seems to happen rather regularly.

So maybe *Homo sapiens* made it to North and South America only 11,000 years ago, or took a telltale dump in Oregon 14,300 years ago, or had genes, which pegged his beginnings here at 17,000 years, and then again maybe it was 40,000 years as Dr. Gonzalez says. Either way, is it really completely out of the ballpark to assert Puma Punktu just might have been built 17,000 years ago, despite archeology's protestations to the contrary?

40,000 year-old human footprint found in Mexico

The Voynich Manuscript

Our archeological museum tour of possible extraterrestrial exhibits is not quite over. We will stop at one more room, this one housing the mysterious Voynich manuscript.

A 235-page text, named after American antique book dealer Wilfrid Voynich, was found in 1912 among a collection of ancient manuscripts kept in a villa near Rome. The manuscript is missing 20 pages, and estimated to have been created in the late 13th century. It contains text and drawings of many unidentified plants, what appear to be herbal recipes, mysterious charts, nudes, and astronomical objects. It is written in a language which has an alphabetic script (see right), variously reckoned to have between 19–28 letters.

This alphabet bears no relationship to any English or European lettering system.

The earliest date to which this text can be affixed is relatively certain, 1586. Emperor Rudolph II in Bohemia purchased it at that time. A letter accompanying the manuscript said that it was the work of Englishman Roger Bacon who lived in the 13th century.

Attempts to decipher it all have failed. Decoding attempts began in earnest after the advances made in cryptography after World War II. A symposium sponsored by the National Security Agency in Washington in 1978 similarly failed to decipher it.

Some computer findings are of interest. For example, one element of professional cryptography known as "Zipf's law" provides statistical criteria to determine if a language or code is a hoax. The Voynich manuscript conforms to standard word frequencies, word repetitions, and appropriate distances between letters and words. These internal consistencies suggest that it is not a hoax, but written in a natural, albeit unknown, language.

Some say that the biological drawings in the text described "asseminiferous tubes, microscopic cells with nuclei, and even spermatozoa," hardly facts known at the time the book was written. Among the astronomical drawings are alleged descriptions of spiral nebulae and a coronary eclipse. [41]

The manuscript has been dubbed the most studied and still the *most mysterious* manuscript in the world. Hundreds of researchers have examined it all with no ultimate resolution. There is today an on-going effort on the internet to decode it. All that is known about it at present is that it is *not related to any known language or any linguistic derivative.* Attempts to link it with Ukrainian, Latin, numerical systems, or European languages have all fallen on their face. One study said that the script appears to be written either by two separate individuals or by one individual at two different parts of his life.

What is most curious to our interest, however, is that one of the diagrams has been likened to a crude drawing of the Milky Way. And in the graphic which follows, the superimposition of one on the other is impressive. So this is either one more lucky coincidence or the author had an uncanny foreknowledge far before any human beings came into possession of such information.

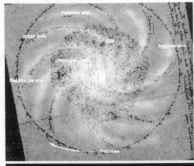
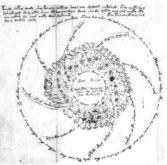
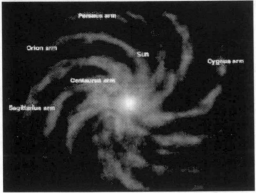

The Voynich manuscript contains a drawing one author likened to a crude depiction of the Milky Way spiral galaxy. When the spiral arms of the galaxy are superimposed on the drawing, it has an uncanny similarity. Author's note: The Voynich manuscript seems to depict 8 arms, however, current astronomical science believes there to be only four. However, if one considers the four arms in rotation, they give the appearance of eight. See the diagram of the Milky Way in . http://en.wikipedia.org/wiki/Milky_Way

It is possible the Voynich manuscript is the work of a highly intelligent schizophrenic in the Dark Ages who created his own language, script, and alphabet. Schizophrenics are known to create fragmentary languages, but one who could make a consistent alphabet, word frequencies, and respect Zipf's law consistently for all 223 pages would mean the schizophrenic was also very gifted.

It could also be the product of a secret alchemical sect, but if so, one would think 21st century CIA decryption, or the National Security Agency, would have decoded it and linked it to some existing language or secret algorithm which would by now have surrendered up its secret codes. The most far-flung hypothesis, of course, is that the reason it has eluded modern cryptography's search for a language to which it might be linked is precisely because the manuscript *has no human linguistic counterpart*, that is, a language unknown on this earth.[42]

Very Recent Archeological Findings

In February, 2010, deep inside a jungle cave in the Hoshangabad district of Madhya Pradesh in India, a strange cave painting was discovered. Although much too early to be fully analyzed by academics, the preliminary interpretations are that this painting shows what appears to the naked eye of a being in some sort of a helmeted space-suit. To those who reported the incident, it also shows . . . "a classical flying saucer shaped UFO that appears to be either beaming something down or beaming something up . . . A force-field or trail of some sort is seen at the rear of the UFO."[43]

Summary

We traveled to the Chinese pyramid mounds, the Giza pyramid plane and then the Thornborough henges in England. We saw curious examples of Egyptian aerodynamics, incredibly accurate Mayan solar calendars, and a mysterious manuscript that has eluded the most sophisticated decryption programs in our modern day arsenals. We considered those gigantic hewn rocks from Lebanon to Peru and strange cross-cultural pyramid planes dotting the globe. We examined two ancient surveys of the mountains and rivers in Antarctica, facts that simply could not possibly have been known and catalogued in recent times—and likely only executed prior to the fourth millennium BC. With that, our archeological tour concludes.

The white pyramid in Xian, China

We are not asserting that ancient astronauts are responsible for these curiosities. Indeed, at this point, we cannot yet decide if this evidence is dubious, persuasive, or conclusive in support of the extraterrestrial hypothesis. We need to look at all the data. That is what the first few introductory chapters of this text are for: data collection.

We will try to connect the dots only after we've lined them up all in a row.

> In 1798, Napoleon Bonaparte embarked on a military expedition of Egypt. Like so many throughout history, he was drawn to the mystique of the Pharaohs. Napoleon was an influential force in the birth of Egyptology. Accompanying his troops were also engineers, surveyors, artists and archaeologists, who were required to document the great ruins of the ancient Egyptian civilization. The inner sanctum of the Pyramids drew Napoleon in, like so many before him and since. After exploring the chambers of Khufu's Great Pyramid, Napoleon requested to be left alone in the King's Chamber. When he finally emerged, he is reported to have been extremely shaken and shocked by something within. When asked what had happened, he refused to discuss it and insisted that the incident never be spoken of again. A friend, who visited Napoleon in his final days, asked him to tell him the secret of that day. Napoleon was ready to speak, but then shook his head and declined. Enigmatically, he responded, "No, what's the use. You'd never believe me." [44]

Endnotes

1 *Feats and Wisdom of the Ancients*: Time-Life, Alexandria, Virginia, 1990.

2 Joseph Jochmans, "Top 10 Out-of-Place Artifacts" Atlantis Rising, #5.

3 See also Lumir Janku, "Ancient Egypt and pre-Columbian airplane models," 1996. source: http://www.bibliotecapleyades.net/esp_aviones_precolom02.htm

4 http://www.bibliotecapleyades.net/piramides/esp_piramides_china_5.htm

5 Temple of the Sun. By: Pérez de Lara, Jorge, *Archaeology*, 00038113, Nov/Dec2005, Vol. 58, Issue 6

6 Hartwig Hausdorf, www.alphaomega.se/english/chinesepry.html.

7 R. Bauval and A. Gilbert, *The Orion Mystery*. New York: Crown, 1994.

8 A recent discovery 20 miles from Cairo unearthed the remains of a 4,000-year-old queen's pyramid. Buried with her were pyramid texts containing special prayers to protect the dead and ensure sustenance in the afterlife. Tanalee Smith, Associated Press, "Rare tomb of queen discovered in Egypt." Cited in *San Jose Mercury News*, April 3, 2000.

9 Christopher Knight & Alan Butler. Before the Pyramids. London: Watkins Publishing, 2009, p. 69

10 Kimua Masaaki, "Age determination of the submarine ruins of Yonaguni Island Okinawa by means of surface irradiation dating method." See http://sciencelinks.jp/j-east/article/200402/000020040203A0851205.php

11 Cited in Hancock, *ibid.*, pp 179-180. It is also said by the third century AD Chinese mathematicians could compute the value of *pi*, and by the fifth century they calculated it to ten decimal places... "a feat unmatched in the West until the sixteenth century." *Feats and Wisdom of the Ancients*: Time-Life, Alexandria, Virginia, 1990.

12 Will Hart. *The Genesis Race*. Rochester VT: Bear & Co.,2003, p77

13 Archeologist Schwaller de Lubicz also was able to demonstrate that the Golden Section was "applied at Luxor and with a complexity and sophistication never achieved by the Greeks." "Pushing back the portals of civilization, J. Douglas Kenyon, in Forbidden History, *Ibid.*, p. 89 Further examples of the Golden Section in the Great Pyramid can be found at Kelly, Paul R.1 Mathematics Teacher; Oct2004, Vol. 98 Issue 3, p206-207, 2p

14 The *Da Vinci Code*, pp 95-96.

15 Cited in Hancock, p. 336.

16 Hancock, *ibid.*, p. 159.

17 The Mayan calendar put the exact length of the year at 365.2420 days. The modern Gregorian calendar puts it at 365.2425 days while the actual duration is 365.2422, making the Mayan calendar more accurate than the one commonly used today. *Feats and Wisdom of the Ancients*: Time-Life, Alexandria, Virginia, 1990.

18 Peter Kosimo, *Not of this World, Ibid.* Note there is some controversy on these calculations. The Great Pyramid's facing stones have been removed over time, so its actual height at construction is an estimate. According to Alaa K. Ashmawy, author of *Seven Wonders of the World*, the height of the Great Pyramid is 146.75 meters. The exact distance to the Sun at perihelion is 147.5 million kilometers. So if one continues to use 1 billion as the multiplier, then multiplying the height of the Great Pyramid gets the perihelion with a margin of error of one half of one percent. In other words, either this is a very lucky coincidence, or the Egyptians built a pyramid encrypting in its structure subtle astronomical and mathematical facts, one of which was that the height of the pyramid predicted the closest distance to the sun with an accuracy of 99.95 percent! (See also http://curious. astro.cornell.edu/question.php?number=582 Also Peter Thompson's *Secrets of the Pyramid*, where the limestone covering on the Great Pyramid which was stripped by vandals was used to estimate the actual height of the pyramid. Although Thompson does not discuss the perihelion, he does argue that its actual height was 147.9 meters, which is consistent with this allegation.) See Peter Thompson, *Secrets of the Great Pyramid*, New York: Galahad books, 1971.

19 Another example of precocity is in Hindu history. It is said that the ancient Hindus knew of the seventh planet, Uranus, long prior to Herschel's discovery of it in AD 1781. See Gods and spacemen in the Ancient East, p. 29, W. Raymond Drake. New York: New American Library, 1973.

20 And if not, then it is clear many had the idea of the earth moving around the sun. Aristarchus of Samos, 1700 years prior to Copernicus, made this discovery as well. *Feats and Wisdom of the Ancients*, Time-Life Books, Alexandria, Virginia, 1990.

21 And in India, "Kananda and the Gnani Yogis speculated on the atom five hundred years before Democritus, Aryabatha in the sixth century before Christ taught the rotation of the Earth, the scientific principles of medicine, botany and chemistry were established as early as 1300 BC in India. Drake, *Ibid.*, p. 63.

22 W. Raymond Drake. *Gods and Spacemen of the Ancient Past*, New York: New American Library, 1974.

23 Source: http://members.tripod.com/-Zomb/ANTARCTI.HTM.

24 Note also that the Oronteus Finaeus maps were originally studied by Dr. Charles Hapgood and Dr. Richard Strachan of MIT. Although Hapgood was treated by disdain by members of his profession, Albert Einstein found his work fascinating.

25 In 1968 the National Science Foundation reported the discovery of a jawbone amphibian some 525 miles from the South Pole, the skeleton of a Labyrinthodont. "An amphibian of this type could only have survived in a hot climate, or at least a warm one, and the report concluded that at one time the Antarctic must have been 'absolutely free of ice'." Some scientists believe that shifts in the earth's crust could explain these findings; findings in Siberia similarly show evidence

of a very warm climatological pattern. Source: Peter Kolosimo, *Not of this World*, ibid., p. 171.

26 The original test evaluating the character of this map is given at http://www. world-mysteries.com/sar_1.htm

27 Graham Hancock, *Fingerprints of the Gods*, New York: Three Rivers Press, p. 30.

28 Vera Solovieva, www.factor-online.com. As an illustration of the vast treasures of knowledge lost to antiquity, it is said that the Egyptian Library in Alexandria in 323 BC possessed ten times the number of volumes that the entirety of Europe possessed in AD 1450. The Library in Alexandria was burned in 46 BC, again in AD 391 and finished off by Arab legions in AD 640.

29 David Childress, *Technology of the Gods*, Kempton, Illinois, Adventures Unlimited Press, 2000, pp. 51-52.

30 Childress, *Ibid.*, p. 57.

31 David Childress, *Ibid.*, p. 45.

32 "Celestial find at ancient Andes site." Thomas Maugh, *Los Angeles Times*, May 14, 2006, p. A28.

33 *Ibid.*

34 Posnansky, A., 1943, *Tihuanacu: the Cradle of American Man.* J. J. Augustin Publisher, New York.

35 "Puma Punktu," Maleeka Spriggs, March 9th, 2009. *Weekly World News.*

36 Great pyramids vs. Puma Punkt, The History Channel: http://www.youtube.com/ watch?v=AABPXvwevVA

37 Haynes, Gary (2002). *The Early Settlement of North America: The Clovis Era.* New York: Cambridge University Press.

38 14,300 years old fossilized feces suggests earliest human presences in North America. *Science News*, April 3, 2008.

39 Bruce Bower, Migrants settle Americas in tandem. *Science News*, Jan. 31, 2009, p. 5.

40 Sources: Alleged 40,000-Year-Old Human Footprints In Mexico Much, Much Older Than Thought *Science Daily* (Dec. 1, 2005); see http://www.sciencedaily. com/releases/2005/11/051130232517.htm.

41 *Voynich Manuscript an Elegant Enigma*—(Cryptographic Series, No 27) by M. E. D'Imperio, M. E. D'Amperio (Paperback - June 1981)and *The Most Mysterious Manuscript*-The Voynich "Roger Bacon" Cipher Manuscript by Robert S. Brumbaugh (Editor). Also see Wikipedia, the free encyclopedia. http: wikipedia.org

42 A recent text reviews the major theories about the manuscript, including the extraterrestrial one. See Lawrence and Nancy Goldstone, *The Friar and the Cipher*, New York, Doubleday, 2005. See also The Voynich Manuscript: The Unsolved Riddle of an Extraordinary Book which Has Defied Interpretation for Centuries," by Gerry Kennedy and Rob Churchill.

43   http://www.archaeologydaily.com/news/201002173333/Prehistoric-UFO-and-ET-images-found-in-remote-cave-in-India.html. The reader should be cau-

tioned that this discovery is so new, it has not been dated, and for all we know it could be contemporary graffiti or a hoax.

44   http://tibetkanagawa.blogspot.com/2006/06/napoleon-mystery-within-pyramid.html

3. MYTHOLOGICAL VISITORS

> *Men came from the stars, knowing everything,*
> *and they examined the four corners of the*
> *sky and the Earth's round surface.*
> —*Mayan Popol Vuh, AD 1524*

There is a garrulous mythological narrative bubbling over with evidence of visitations from other worlds. The notion of individuals rising up into the heavens or creatures who descend from the heavens is absolutely pandemic. So prolific is this body of evidence, we will just excerpt its most important elements.

The *Ramayana*, the great Indian epic poem dating from the third century BC:

> ... describes a double-deck circular aircraft with port holes and a dome—a configuration reminiscent of twentieth-century flying saucer reports. Fueled by a strange yellowish white liquid, the craft was said to travel at the speed of wind, attain heights that made the ocean look like a small pool of water, and stop and hover motionless in the sky.[1]

From ancient India come other accountings:

In his battles Indra was attended by the Maruts or Storm Gods, depicted as youthful warriors, who rode on golden cars; they brandished darts of lightning in their hands and drove like the winds. Associated with Indra was Vayu, God of the Wind, who sped across the sky faster than light in a shining chariot drawn by a pair of ruddy steeds with eyes like the sun. Savitri, the Sun God, was borne by swift courses spanning the heavens and beaming inspiration to men. Vishnu traverses the three worlds in three strides and Pushan, the 'best pilot of the air, cut the void with dazzling swiftness for another solar deity, Surya. In the Konarak, India, are found the finest carvings of the Eight Wheels described as a transportation for the Sun Goddess, Surya, to the sky. The most frequently invoked Gods were the twin Aswins, who drove a ruddy, tawny car, bright as burnished gold, armed with thunderbolts; sometimes they 'floated over the ocean, keeping out the water' in a vehicle oddly described as 'tri-columnar, triangular and trip-wheeled, well constructed' on which they rescued Bhujya from the sea in a ship which flew from space.[2]

From the Mahabarata:

Bhima flew with his Vimana on an enormous ray, which had the brilliance of the sun and whose noise was like the thunder of a storm.[3]

In the Caroline Isles,

. . . natives of the Caroline Isles in their *Haida Texts* describe wondrous beings in flying-machines shaped like discs, who descended to Earth and taught their ancestors centuries ago.[4]

Japanese tradition is documented in a relic dated to 670 BC. It was Japanese in origin but translated by the Chinese, who called it the Nihongi. The *Nihongi* tells how

...the Emperor Kami-Yamato-Iharo-Biko spoke with his celestial forefathers who had then gone home on board an oscillating celestial vessel and going back in time for over one million seven hundred and ninety-two thousand four hundred and seventy years.[5]

The City of the Gods in Teotihuacan, Mexico, was a place where once-buried men turned into gods. These pyramids were "the place where men became gods."

Similarly, in Egypt:

[the] archaic hieroglyphs of the Pyramid Texts, the oldest coherent body of writing in the world, left little room for doubt that the ultimate objective of the rituals carried out within those colossal structures was to bring the deceased pharaoh's transfiguration—to "throw open the doors of the firmament and to make a road" so that he might "ascend into the company of the gods."[6]

Mayan sarcophagus thought by some to depict a Mayan god sitting at the controls of a mysterious engine whose fiery exhaust emerges at the bottom of his chair

Such coincidences from culture to culture—or pyramid to pyramid—show a rather universal mythology about men ascending to or descending from the heavens.

RUKMA VIMANA

Instructions on the construction of a mercury engine rocket say:

Strong and durable must the body of the Vinana be made, like a great flying bird of light material. Inside one must put the mercury engine with its iron heating apparatus underneath. By means of the power latent in the mercury which sets the driving whirlwind in motion, a man sitting inside may travel a great distance in the sky. The movements of the Vinana are such that it can vertically ascend, vertically descent, move slanting forwards and backwards. With the help of the machines human beings can fly in the air and heavenly beings can come down to earth. (Source: atributetohinduism.com)

From a translation of the ancient work *Samar*, there is a description of flying machines.

The aerial cars are made of light wood like a great bird with a durable and well-formed body having mercury inside and fire at the bottom. It has two resplendent wings and is propelled by air. It flies in the atmospheric regions for a great distance and carries several persons with it. The inside construction resembles heaven created by Brahma himself.[7]

Elsewhere in India,

... the Asura (non-God) called Maya owned an animated golden car with four strong wheels and having a circumference of 12,000 cubits, which possessed the wonderful power of flying at will to any place. Dikshitar states this car was equipped with various weapons and bore huge standards in the battle between the Devas and the Asuras in which Mayha distinguished himself; several warriors were said to have ridden birds.[8] [9]

Again from India, the Mysore International Academy of Sanskrit reports:

The manuscripts we present in translation from Sanskrit describe various types of automatic ships adapted for travel on land, sea, or in air and from planet to planet. It seems that they could stop still in the sky and even become invisible.[10]

From ancient Egypt:

A badly decayed papyrus among the papers of the deceased Professor Alberto Tulli, Director of the Egyptian Museum of the Vatican was identified as part of the Annals of Thutmosis III about 1500 BC:
... In the year 22, of the 3rd month of winter, sixth hour of the day, the scribes of the House of Life found that there was a circle of fire coming from the sky ... it had no head. From its mouth came a breath that stank. One rod long was its body and a rod wide, and it was noiseless. And the hearts of the scribes became terrified and confused, and they laid themselves flat on their bellies ... They reported to the Pharaoh. His Majesty ... was medi-

tating on what had happened and which is recorded in papyri of the House of Life. Now after some days had gone by, behold these things became more numerous in the skies than ever. They shone more than the brightness of the sun, and extended to the limits of the four supports of the heavens. Dominating in the sky was the station of these fire circles. The army of the Pharaoh looked on with him in their midst. It was after supper. Thereupon these fire circles ascended higher in the sky towards the south. Fishes and winged animals or birds fell down from the sky. A marvel never before known since the foundation of this land! And Pharaoh caused incense to be brought to make peace on earth ... And what happened was ordered by the Pharaoh to be written in the annals for the House of Life ... so that it be remembered forever. [11]

And from Babylon,

In excavations in Nineveh there was discovered in the Library of King Assurbanipal, clay cylinders on which is described a voyage to the sky. It narrates how King Etan, who lived about five thousand years ago, called "the Good King," was taken as a feted guest on a flying ship in the form of a shield, which landed in a square behind the royal palace, rotating, surrounded by a vortex of flames. From the flying ship alighted tall blond men with dark complexions dressed in white, handsome as Gods, who invited King Etan, somewhat dissuaded by his own advisers, to go for a trip in the flying ship; in the middle of a whirlwind of flames and smoke he went so high that the Earth with its seas, islands, continents, appeared to him like "a loaf in a basket" then disappeared from sight. King Etan in the flying ship reached the Moon, Mars, Venus, and after two weeks absence, when they were already preparing a new succession to the throne, believing that the Gods had carried him off with them, the flying ship glided over the city and touched down surrounded by a ring of fire. The fire abated, King Etan descended with some of the blond men who stayed as his guest for some days.[12]

From Africa,

The Shilluk people of the Upper Nile believe that the first kings were ... sons of the supreme ruler who flew away from Earth and occupied the divine throne. Bushman mythology reports that its first kings (chiefs) were the sons (Cogaz and Gewi) of Kaang who left Earth to go to their abode at "the top of the sky."[13]

From Eskimo culture comes another accounting:

The first men were much bigger than present-day men. They could fly with their magic house, and the snow shovels moved of their own accord and shoveled the snow alone. If the people of that age wanted different kind for food, they simply went into their flying houses and flew to a new place . . . In those days snow could burn like fire and fire often fell from heaven.[14]

From American Indian culture, we hear the following account:

The Haida Indians in the Queen Charlotte Islands [British Columbia] . . . retain the tradition of "great sages descended from the stars on discs of fire," while the Navajos tell of 'creatures who came from the sky and stayed a long time on Earth but finally returned to their world."[15]

From the Indian subcontinent taken from the *Bhagavata Purana*:

The Gods came in their respective flying vehicles to witness the battle between Kripacarya and Arjuna. Even Indra, the Lord of Heaven, came with a special type of flying vehicle which could accommodate 33 divine beings.[16]

And elsewhere in these Indian texts:

The King is a flame, moving before the wind to the end of the sky and to the end of the earth . . . the King travels the air and traverses the earth . . . there is brought to him a way of ascent to the sky.[17]

In Sumeria,

In Ancient Sumer clay tablets describe visits of the gods. The gods fly in vehicles, called Shems, or Mu, which are described as being tall rocket like "rocks" from which fire flies. The visiting gods stay at temples, built by humans under the instructions of the gods, and are waited on.[18]
Elsewhere in Sumeria Emmeduranki, the prince of Sippa was "taken to an orbiting craft and taught science and math."[19]

Then, of course, we have biblical sources:

Thessalonians 4:17 Then we which are alive and remain shall be caught up together with them in the clouds, to meet the Lord in the air: and so shall we ever be with the Lord.

Revelation: 11:11 And after three days and a half, the spirit of life from God entered into them, and they stood upon their feet; and great fear fell upon them which was them. And they heard a great voice from heaven saying unto them. Come up hither. And they ascended up to heaven in a cloud; and their enemies beheld them.

Acts 1:9 And when he had spoken these things, while they beheld, he was taken up; and a cloud received him out of their sight.

Kings 2:1 And it came to pass, when the Lord would take up Elijah into heaven by a whirlwind, that Elijah went with Elisha from Gilgal.

Again in Kings 2:11 It came to pass, as they still went on, and talked, that behold, there appeared a chariot of fire, and horses of fire, and parted them both asunder; and Elijah went up by a whirlwind into heaven.

Ezekiel 10:16 And when the cherubim's went, the wheels went by them: and when the cherubim lifted up their wings to mount up from the earth, the same wheels also turned not from beside them.

Revelation 7:2 And I saw another angel ascending from the east, having the seal of the living God: and he cried with a loud voice to the four angels.

In the Apocrypha, Noah and Enoch "were reported to have been taken into space."[20] But in the Judeo-Christian Bible, there is probably no more explicit an accounting than the story of Ezekiel.

Ezekiel

This passage is said to have been written about six hundred years before Christ and is quoted in its entirety:

I looked, and I saw a windstorm coming out of the north—and immense cloud with flashing lightning and surrounded by brilliant light. The center of the fire looked like glowing metal, and in the fire was what looked like four living creatures. In appearance their form was that of a man, but each of them had four faces and four wings. Their legs were straight; their feet were like those of a calf and gleamed like burnished bronze. Under their wings on their four sides they had the hands of a man. All four of them had faces and wings, and their wings touched one another. Each one went straight ahead; they did not turn as they moved (1:4-9).

Their faces looked like this: each of the four had the face of a man, and on the right side each had the face of a lion, and on the left the face of an ox; each also had the face of an eagle. Such were their faces. Their wings were spread out upward; each had two wings, one touching the wing of another creature on either side, and two wings covering its body. Each one went straight ahead. Wherever the spirit would go, they would go, without turning as they went. The appearance of the living creatures was like burning coals of fire or like torches; it was bright, and lightning flashed out of it. The creatures sped back and forth like flashes of lightning (1:20-14).

As I looked at the living creatures, I saw a wheel on the ground beside each creature with its four faces. This was the appearance and structure of the wheels. They sparkled like chrysolite, and all four looked alike. Each appeared to be made like a wheel intersecting a wheel. As they moved, they would go in any one of the four directions the creatures faced; the wheels did not turn about as the creatures went. Their rims were high and awesome, and all four rims were full of eyes all around (1:15:18).

Depiction of Ezekiel's vision

When the living creatures moved, the wheels beside them moved; and when the living creatures rose from the ground, the wheels also rose. Wherever the spirit would go, they would go, and the wheels would rise along with them, because the spirit of the living creatures was in the wheels. When the creatures moved, I heard the sound of their wings, like the roar of the Almighty, like the tumult of an army (1:19-20, 24).

The Dogon

Accounts of extraterrestrial contacts, perhaps misinterpreted by ancients as "God" or "Gods," infect countless mythological systems. One of the more curious mythic systems is from the Dogon in Mali, West Africa.

. . . The Dogon are believed to be of Egyptian descent and their astronomical lore goes back to 3200 BC. According to their traditions, the star Sirius *has a companion star*, which is invisible to the naked eye.

This companion star has a 50-year elliptical orbit around the visible Sirius and is extremely heavy. It also rotates on its axis. This legend might be of little interest to anybody but two French anthropologists, Marcel Griaule and Germain Dieterlen who recorded it from four Dogon priests in the 1930s. Of little interest *except that it is exactly true*. How did a people who lacked any kind of astronomic devices know so much about an invisible star? The star, which scientists call Sirius B, wasn't even photographed until 1970 by a large telescope.

According to their oral traditions, a race of people from the Sirius system called the Nommos visited Earth thousands of years ago. The Nommos were ugly, amphibious beings that resembled mermen and mermaids. They also appear in Babylonian, Accadian, and Sumerian myths. The Egyptian Goddess Isis, who is sometime depicted as a mermaid, is also linked with the star Sirius.

The Nommos, according to the Dogon legend, lived on a planet that orbits another star in the Sirius system. They landed on Earth in an "ark" that made a spinning descent to the ground with great noise and wind. It was the Nommos that gave the Dogon the knowledge about Sirius B.

The legend goes on to say the Nommos also furnished the Dogons with some interesting information about our own solar system: That the planet Jupiter has major moons, that Saturn has rings, that the planets orbit the sun. These were all facts discovered by Westerners only after Galileo invented the telescope. The story of the Dogon and their legend was brought to popular attention by Robert Temple in a book published in 1977 called the *Sirius Mystery*.

Carl Sagan pooh-poohed this idea by conjecturing that the Dogon had contact with Westerners and may have confabulated their oral history.[21] A second skeptic argues similarly. Nonetheless it doesn't seem to explain a 400-year old Dogon artifact that apparently depicts the Sirius configuration nor the ceremonies held by the Dogon since the 13th century to celebrate the cycle of Sirius A *and B*.

Clearly the Dogons have an elaborate record of visitations by others, which they memorialized in ritual over the centuries—and they did not believe the earth was flat, either! The accuracy of these ancient testimonials is, of course, less of interest than the fact of their very existence.

Interbreeding with the Gods

Perched on our tree of mythological evidence is another branch hosting another yet another kind of fruit, the cross-cultural narrative which describes God, Gods, spirits, and peoples from other lands who descend to earth and interact with earthlings. From Hindu, Tibetan, Iroquois, Mexican, Mesopotamian, Greek, Roman, Hawaiian, Chinese, Russian, Finnish, Teutonic, and African cultures, the listing of sky gods and creatures who ascended or descended from the heavens, who consorted with man, and may have bred with mortal man is immense. Here is a partial list of sixty-one such entities: [22]

Viracocha, the creator god in Inca mythology.

In Egypt . . .

The oldest kings belong to the great Ennead, a family of nine deities. These deities multiplied offspring on this earth. They are succeeded as kings by a number of monarchs described as demigods. After this, a number of broken lines conclude with the followers of Horus, or exalted spirits, or heroes, the immediate predecessors of the first historical dynasty somewhat before 3999 BC. The king was chosen by the god Tem or the god Amen. The kings on the throne of Egypt believed in all seriousness that they had divine blood in their veins and they acted as they thought gods would act.[23]

Table 3.1 Sky Gods

Aditi	Khawandagar	Nut
Amayicoyon	Hannahanna	Odin
Anatu	Hephaestus	Olorum
Anu	Hathor	Qamaits
Apollo	Hebat	Poseidon
Ares	Heitsi	Quetzatcoatl
Artemis	Hestia	Rangi
Athena	Hera	Rugaha
Azer-Ava	Horus	Saule
Ay-Ayec	Innana	Thor
Bau	Inti	Tammuz
Demeter	Jaqta	Unl
Diana	Jarilo	Unkulunkulu
Dionysus	Jesus	Vaya
DiJun	Maia	Viracocha
Dnar	Marduk	Wawalag
Dumuzi	Mawa	Xbalanque
Dyausa	Mayaheul	Zeus
Estanathehi	Mehturt	
Enlil	Min	
Geezhigo	Mitra	
Gukumatz	Nambi	
Hannahanna		

In Sumeria we have a similar story:

After Anu, Enlil, Enki and Ninhursag had fashioned the black-headed people, animals were brought artfully into existence. After kingship had been lowered from heaven, the Immortals perfected the ordinances, founded the cities, apportioned them their rulers, established the cleaning of the small rivers.

What the Immortals are said to be doing here is setting up a society. They modified the people, domesticated cereals and animals, provided equipment. Then they established kings to rule for them. Finally came the divine laws, their regulations governing these mortals in the built-up areas:

We can see that the Mesopotamians were convinced that they received civilization as gift from the gods, and this is the way to understand kingship coming down from heaven.[24]

In Japan,

The . . . Japanese bask in the belief that their earliest ancestors came from 'the Abode of the Gods,' and worship their Mikado as direct descendant of Amaterasu, the shining Goddess of the Sun, Ruler of the High Plains of Heaven.[5]

And in *Genesis:*

The sons of God saw that the daughters of men were beautiful; and they took wives for themselves, whoever they chose. [6:2]

In the words of W. Raymond Drake:

Indra flashed over Old India in an aerial car drawn by steeds with golden man and shining skin. Padma Sambhava soared to Tibetan skies in a marvelous tent. Celestials in China flew on fiery dragons. The Honorable Gods descended to Japan in Heavenly Rocking Boats: Horus waged aerial warfare over Egypt in his Divine Eye; Ashur of Babylon sped through the air in a winged disk. Zeus raced across the heavens in a winged chariot. Woden drove a star wagon. Keridwen flew down to Wales in a car drawn by winged dragons. Quetzalcoatl visited Mexico on a fiery serpent, Viracocha winged down to Peru on a giant condor; the Red Indians believed the Great spirit flew on the Thunderbird.[26]

H. Sapiens records of immortals, Gods, and beings descending to earth, or ascending to another world is prolific, and their having mated with man almost as ubiquitous.

> A whole sequence of such creation myths are found in Africa as well. The Nyoro believe God sent the first human couple down from heaven when he established the world. Kivu pygmies believe the progenitor of man came from heaven as do the Kuluwe. In Nigeria the Yoruba believe the sky god Oldumare came from heaven to create man.[27] The Bena-Lulua say that God sent his four sons down to earth. The Ashanti say god created seven men who came down to earth from heaven. They produced men here and then returned to heaven.[28]

We can remind ourselves here that in the Genesis myth, God fashioned Man as well. Even in the so-called apocryphal texts that are not part of the accepted versions of the Christian Bible like the Book of Enoch, there are continuing references to his genetic meddling with humankind.

> When the sons of men multiplied in those days daughters were born of them, elegant and beautiful. And when the angels, the sons of heaven had seen them they fell in love with them and said to each other: 'Let us choose women of the race of men and have sons by them.[29]

Indeed there are even stories of breeding experiments with humans which went awry.

> And the daughters of Cain *with whom the angels had companied conceived,* but they were unable to bring forth their children, and they died. And of the children who were in their wombs some died, and some came forth.[30]

Were we actually visited by extraterrestrials, or is all this data dismissed as merely wish fulfillment, analgesic illusion, and histrionic folk lore which give a people a sense of importance that they were selected or chosen by God? We will attempt an answer in a later chapter, but for the present, there is yet more data to gather in properly preparing our database:

Laws from Heaven

There is a pervasive set of myths about laws of conduct being passed down from the heavens to earthlings to govern their behavior. Because we tend to be most influenced by Judeo-Christian thinking, the Ten Commandments as handed to Moses atop Mount Sinai is our singular sense that our behavioral code is based on the highest authority.

But other cultures have similar notions, testimony of the ubiquity of this concept. Zoroaster received the laws of Persia from Ahura-Mazda on Mount Sabalan. And he isn't the only Moses proxy:

> Believers in the Scriptures should know that Minos, the Founder of Knossos, received the Cretan law from a God on a sacred mountain, [quoted by Dionysius of Halicarnasus in Roman Antiquities, 2-61.] . . . A stele unearthed at Babylon depicts Hammurabi, the great Lawgiver, accepting his famous laws on tablets of stone from the God, Shamash, also on a mountain. Most countries venerate some holy mountain associated with their Gods. [31]

In fact the notion of sacred mountains where man connects to Gods in the heavens covers the planet rather handily. [32] See Table 3.2.

Tutors

Not only is ancient mythology filled with sky gods and their flying machines, plus an ample supply of interbreeding stories, but myriad myths deal with extraterrestrial tutelage, moral education—commandments—and scientific education.

Table 3.2 Gods and Sacred Mountains

Mountain	Religion/Culture	Location
Mt. Atlas	Ancient Greeks	Greece
Mt. Waka	Incas	Peru
Mt. Ausangati	Incas	Peru
Mt. Tepeyac	Aztecs	Mexico
Mt. Olympus	Greeks	Greece
Mt. Sinai	Jewish/Christian	Egypt
Mt. Arafat	Jewish/Christian	Turkey
Mt.Adam	Hindu/Buddhist	Sri Lanka
Kang Rimpoche	Hindu/Buddhist	Tibet
Machapuchare	Hindu/Buddhist	Tibet
Everest	Hindu/Buddhist	India
Kilauea	Native Hawaiian	Hawaii
Mt. Athos	Greek	Greece
Fujiyama	Japanese folk	Japan
Mt. Meru	Hindu	Mesopotamia
Himinbjorg	Scandinavian folk	Scandinavia
Thabor	Muslim	Palestine
Meru	Hindu	India
Mt of the rising sun	Sumerian folk	Iraq
Montserrat	Pre-Christian	Catalonia
Mount Hara	Zoroastrian	Iran

These, of course, are a mere sampling, but one important observation from scholar Paul Von Ward is worth noting: "In an extensive review of documented world myths, I have not discovered a single story that portrays the founding of its civilization resulting from the *unaided* efforts of humans. They never say this or that human did that, or even discovered it . . ."[33]

Table 3.3 Sky Gods and Their Pedagogy

Sky god credited	People	Innovation
Manaboshu	Cheppews	Bow & arrow/ copper
Gluskap	Algonquins	General education
Quetzalcoatl	Toltec	Calendars/maize
Fria	Frisian	Moral laws
Enoch	Azerbaijan	General education
Nagas	India	Naviation, military principles, and architecture.
Solon	Greeks	Cosmology, divination, medicine, and law
Thoth	Egypt	Writing, arithmetic, architecture, surveying, geometry, astronomy, medicine, and surgery
Viracocha	Incas	Agriculture, general knowledge
Juok	Africa	Raising cattle and millet
Tsohanoai	Navajo	weapons
Hercules	Greek	Magnetic compass
Typhon	Romans	Magnetic compass
Harveri	Egypt	Compass
Phos	Greek	Use of fire
Hermes	Greek	Written language
Taut	Phoenician	Written language
Sarasvati	India	Written language
Gukamatz	Maya	Codes of law, agriculture, fishing and medicine.

Table based in part on Paul VonWard's *Gods, Genes, and Consciousness*, Hampton Roads, 2004, pp150-184. See also http://www.statemaster.com/encyclopedia/Gukumatz.

Rarely are human innovators themselves extolled and praised in ancient texts and tablets. Only the gods seem to be credited with a footnote. This tradition syncopates throughout ancient society and is found in *Genesis*, with the Dakota Indians, Sioux, Chinese, Eskimos, Mayans, Ethiopians, Persians, Egyptians, and Japanese.

Summing Up

If we go back to our original metaphor—the bullied third grade boy and his *T. Rex* nightmare—just as his dream image pointed to something, we can wonder whether all of these mythological wanderings with the Gods points to something too.

If we were to tease out the sub-text from these ubiquitous myths, what filters through seems to be two-fold: (1) Creatures from the stars visited us. (2) They engaged in a kind of pedagogy with us or something even more serious: co-mingling, marriage, or selective breeding, and our relationship to them may be consanguineal.

Sure this could all be wish fulfillment and delusion providing our species a heavenly veneer it doesn't deserve, but it is also possible that what drives these archetypal narratives are actual archaic memories of visitations by extraterrestrials . . . as if our mythologies provide a mnemonic that helps recall important events in the history of our species.

Our birth is but a sleep and a forgetting:
The Soul that rises with us, our life's Star,
Hath had elsewhere its setting,
And cometh from afar.
—Wordsworth

*Gukumatz was a culture hero who taught the Toltecs,
and later the Maya, the arts of civilization, including codes of law,
agriculture, fishing and medicine. He came from an ocean, and
eventually returned to it. According to Mayan legend, Gukumatz will
return to the Earth . . .*
—Nation Master encyclopedia

*He had the feet of a man, and the tail of a fish; and his speech
and voice resembled that of a man . . . . This monster dwelt by day with
men, but took no food; he gave them knowledge of letters, arts, and
sciences; he taught them to build towers and temples; and to establish
laws; he instructed them in the principles of geometry; taught them
to sow, and to gather the fruits of the earth; in short, whatever could
contribute to polish and civilize their manners. At sun set he retired
to the sea, in which he passed the night. There appeared likewise others
of the same species.*

—Babylonian writer Berossus, who composed
The History of Babylonia, 290 BC [34]

Endnotes

1 *Feats and Wisdom of the Ancients*: Time-Life, Alexandria, Virginia, 1990.

2 Raymond Drake, *Ibid.*, *Gods and Spacemen in the Ancient East*, p. 33.

3 Roy Podtrap Chandra, *The Mahabharata*, Calcutta, 1891.

4 W. Raymond Drake, *Ibid.*, p. 225.

5 Peter Kolosimo, *Ibid.*, p 222.

6 Hancock, *Ibid.*, p. 168

7 Drake, ibid, p.40.

8 Drake, *ibid.*, p. 50; citing the Drona Parva, p. 145.

9 Some of these texts even say how the aerial cars ran: "Strong and durable must the body be made, like a great flying bird, of light material. Inside it one must place the mercursy-injection with its iron heating apparatus beneath. By means of the power latent in the mercury which sets the driving whirlwind in motion, a man sitting inside may travel a great distance in the sky in a most marvelous manner." Source: Childress, *ibid.*, p. 175.

10 Peter Kolosimo, *ibid.*, pp. 43-44.

11 W. Raymond Drake, *ibid.*, pp. 172-173.

12 W. Raymond Drake quoting Alberto Fenoglio in *Clypeus*, *ibid.*, p. 180.

13 *Gods, Genes & Consciousness*, *ibid.*, p. 187.

14 Peter Freudhen, *Book of the Eskimos*, London, 1962.

15 Peter Kolosimo, *ibid.*, p. 65.

16 Cited in Hancock, *ibid.*, p. 489

17 Cited in Hancock, *ibid.*, p. 489.

18 http://www.ufoevidence.org/documents/doc175.htm.

19 *Gods, Genes, & Consciousness*, *ibid.*, p. 25.

20 *Gods, Genes, & Consciousness*, *ibid.*, p. 25.

21 McDaid, Liam Skeptic; 2004, Vol. 11 Issue 1, p40-42, 3p

22 http://en.wikipedia.org/wiki/Life-death-rebirth_deity. Some data also comes from Paul Von Ward, Gods, Genes, &Consciousness, Hampton Roads, 2004.

23 Gardiner, Sir Alan, *Egypt of the Pharaohs*, London, OUP 1978 Book I pages 1-3, abridged, Book III page 420 abridged

24 Lambert, W.G. & Millard, A.R., Atrahasis, *The Babylonian Flood Story and the Sumerian Flood Story* by M. Civil, Oxford, The Clarendon Press, 1969, page 18, excerpt, amended.

25 W. Raymond Drake, *Gods and Spacemen in the Ancient East*, New York, New American Library, 1973, p. 88.

26 Sons of God has proved difficult for biblical scholars. In Genesis there is a problem with the sons of god (plural) and also the term 'Nephilim.' "The Nephilim were on the earth in those days, and also afterward when the sons of God came in to the daughter of men, and they bore children to them." Genesis 6:4.

27 *The Origin of Life and Death: African Creation Myths*, Ulli Beier (ed.). London: Heinmann, 1966.

28 Baumann Hermann, *Schopfung und Urzeit des Menschen im Mythos der Afrikanischen*. Volker, Berlin, 1936.

29 Cited in Peter Kolosimo, *Not of this World*, Milan, Souvenir Press, 1970, p. 27.

30 Andrew Collins. *From the Ashes of Angels*: Vermont: Bear & Co, 2001, p. 35.

31 W. Raymond Drake, *ibid.*, p. 171. Elsewhere Drake alleges that Zoroaster and Mohammed also communed with celestials on mountains (see p. 211).

32 Carlos Fernandez-Baca Tupayachi. *Saqsaywaman: A Model of Atlantis*, 2006, Biblioteca Nacional del Peru.

33 Paul Von Ward, *Gods, Genes and Consciousness*, Virginia: Hampton Roads, 2004, pp160-162.

34 http://www.oannes.com/ The original text where this translation appears is Isaac Preston Cory, *Ancient Fragments of the Phoenician, Chaldean, Egyptian...* Second Edition. London: William Pickering, 1832.

4. PARANORMAL EVIDENCE FOR EXTRATERRESTRIAL CONTACT: UFOs

Yes, I know they exist. Now talk to me about
what all this means.[1]
—CIA Director, James Woolsey, Dec. 13, 1993, in a
private conversation about UFOs.

I can assure you that flying saucers, given that they exist, are
not constructed by any power on earth.[2]
—President Harry S. Truman

The phenomenon of UFOs does exist, and it
must be treated seriously.
—Mikhail Gorbachev, *Soviet Youth*, May 4, 1990.[3]

Flying saucers are real. Too many good men have seen them,
that don't have hallucinations.[4]
— Captain Edward 'Eddie' Rickenbacker (1890–1973)

If we are to give a full court summary of evidence regarding the extraterrestrial hypothesis, we need to look at what is commonly called the 'paranormal,' and here I am referring to UFO literature and more recent literature on crop circles. This is a much more speculative body of data, so let us begin as conservatively as we can.

One U.S. government document published in 1965 concludes that after 18 years of UFO study, there were at least 663 sightings, which could not be dismissed. "What is certain is that these things were not test balloons lost in the sky; neither were they light refraction phenomena, or stars, aircraft, missiles or flying objects of man-made or known physical origin."[5]

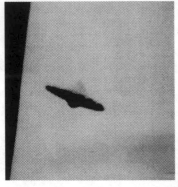

UFO photo taken from car window in Pueblo, NM

Apart from private conversations and off-the-record comments, this is as close as the government ever got to officially admitting UFOs might exist. That isn't much.

There are many UFO stories throughout recorded history. On a papyrus of Pharaoh Thutmose III who ruled Egypt from 1468 to 1436 BC a ship strongly resembling a UFO is reported.[6]

Saint Bede, known as the father of English history, writes in his *Historia Ecclesiastica Gentis Anglorum* of an event, which occurred in the year AD 664. He observed a huge light which came down from the sky, settled a while near the abbey, finally disappearing into the depths of space. He described the light as so strong it made sunlight seem pale in comparison.[7]

A curious event occurs in Aurora, Texas in 1897. Remember, this was before airplanes. The local paper reported the event as follows:

> About six o'clock this morning the early risers of Aurora were astonished at the sudden appearance of the airship which has been sailing through the country. It was traveling due north, and much nearer the earth than before. Evidently some of the machinery was out of order, for it was making a speed of only ten or twelve miles an hour and gradually settling toward the earth. It waded over the public square and when it reached the north part of town, collided with the tower of Judge Proctor's

windmill and went to pieces with a terrific explosion, scattering debris over several acres of ground, wrecking the windmill and water tank and destroying the judge's flower garden. The pilot of the ship is supposed to have been the only one aboard, and while his remains are badly disfigured, enough of the original has been picked up to show that he was not an inhabitant of this world. Mr. T.J. Seens, the U.S. Signal Service officer at this place and an authority on astronomy gives it his opinion that he was a native of the planet Mars. Papers found on his person—evidently the records of his travels—are written in some unknown hieroglyphics and cannot be deciphered. The ship was too badly wrecked to form any conclusion as to its construction or mode of power. It was built of an unknown metal, resembling somewhat a mixture of aluminum and silver, and it must have weighed several tons. The town today is full of people who are viewing the wreckage and gathering specimens of strange metal from the debris. The pilot's funeral will take place a noon tomorrow.

Signed: E.E. Hayden.

Subsequently researchers located the graveyard in Aurora, and while an unmarked gravestone was found, the body was gone.[8]

Rarely do governments validate the appearance of UFOs following some arcane rule that official entities should always suppress or reframe any such sightings. However, in 1965 the Argentinean government was miraculously derelict in this obligation and reported a sighting as follows:

The naval garrison in the Argentinean Antarctic noticed on July 3rd at 19:14 hours a huge lens shaped flying object; it seemed to be solid, of a reddish-green color chiefly, sometimes changing to a yellow, blue, white or orange shade. The object moved in a zig-zag towards the east, but changed course several times towards the west and north at varying speeds and quite silently, passing at 45 degrees over the horizon at a distance of 10 to 15 kilometers from the base . . . In the course of the movement completed by the object itself, it was possible for the eye-witnesses to get some idea of its enormous speed . . . because it was poised motionless for about 15 minutes at a height of around 5,000 meters.[9]

Some 25 million Americans, approximately 10 percent of the population, report they have seen UFOs, and 57 percent believe they are real.[10] However, there are many scientific problems with UFO reports and sightings, ancient or modern. They suffer from being anecdotal and singular reports not commonly experienced by large numbers of witnesses. Secondly, the photographic evidence, so often impressive, is easily faked, particularly in the digital age, making verification and validation impugnable.

There are a few incidents however, which are slightly more immune from these criticisms, so we will look at these in greater detail as examples of 'best evidence.'

Roswell, 1947[11]

The tale of the crash landing of aliens in Roswell, New Mexico in 1947, if true, would be the most significant news item of the last two millennia, and proof that not only other civilizations exist, but that we made contact. Here is a brief synopsis of the event and its fifty-year history:

In early July, 1947 a rancher named William "Mac" Brazel came to the sheriff's office in Roswell and said he had found some unusual debris. He thought it might be from 'one of those flying saucers.' Marcel and another military man, under the direction of the base commander, Col. William Blanchard, accompanied Brazel to his ranch and found unusual paper-backed foil, balsa struts, some Bakelite-like material, and markings which was "something decipherable like Chinese or hieroglyphic writing."

After returning to the base, Blanchard directed the issuance of a press announcement saying the US Army had recovered one of the mysterious flying disks. The headline gathered national attention.

Then in quick succession Brig. Gene Roger Ramen announced it was a case of mistaken identity. Brazel was held at the guest house on the base and not allowed to go home. 'It was like being in prison,' he remarked. Secretly, General Schulgen, chief of the Air Force Requirements Division, asked J. Edgar Hoover to assist in the matter of flying disks and reported to him "the disks do not originate from earth."

Four bodies were allegedly recovered as well.

The owner of Radio KGFL which was reporting this story received phone calls from Clinton Anderson, Congressman for New Mexico, and Senator Dennis Chavez both threatening to withdraw his broadcasting license if he transmitted an interview he had with Brazel. Radio KGFL was told point blank "Do not broadcast or lose your license!"

Meanwhile a team of experts arrived from Washington and the wreck loaded on to a plane. The pilot, Capt. Oliver Henderson maintained he saw 3 ET bodies still in the hangar stored in ice. At lunchtime Glenn Dennis met the nurse from the base. She told him she had assisted in the autopsies, which were carried out by two doctors from Washington on three little beings—they had big heads, sunken eyes, and four fingers.

According to one debunker, the incident resulted from a downed 657 foot tall flight and instrumentation array launched from nearby Alamogordo Army Air Field in support of a highly classified army air force research and development project code named Mogul.

Information supporting the accuracy of these accounts however, comes from many sources. The information officer, Maj. Jess Marcel, who said originally that he was required to say that there was a big error and the disk merely a weather balloon later said in retirement (1980) that a disk had indeed crashed at Roswell. Walter Haut, the press officer, who allowed the flying saucer story to first go out and later altered it to say it was a weather balloon, also confessed in retirement (1996) the weather balloon story was merely a cover.[12]

Walter Haut

In the early 1980s Jaime Shandera was a producer in Los Angeles working under Bill Moore on a UFO story. Moore, in turn, was working with scientist Stanton Friedman. Someone left a mysterious set of documents under Shandera's door. These were marked top secret and in the course of this history have become known as the MJ documents. They could easily be forgeries, of course, but they are baffling in their level of detail.

Allegedly prepared for President Eisenhower in 1952 and labeled Top Secret For Your Eyes Only, they identify the Roswell matter as Operation Majestic 12, and list its supervising members of the Roswell study group as Adm. Roscoe Hillenkoetter, Dr. Vannevar Bush, Secretary Forrestal, and others. Here are some quotations from this document. If true, these excerpts would constitute one of the most revolutionary documents since the New Testament.

> On 07 July 1947 a secret operation was begun to assure recovery of the wreckage of this object for scientific study. During the course of the operation, aerial reconnaissance discovered that four small human-like beings had apparently ejected from the craft at some point before it exploded. These had fallen to earth about two miles east of the wreckage site. All four were dead and badly decomposed due to action by predators and exposure to the elements during the approximately one week time period which had elapsed before their discovery . . . the wreckage of the craft was also removed to several different locations. Civilian and military witnesses in the area were debriefed, and news reporters were given the effective cover story that the object had been a misguided weather research balloon.[13]
> The disk was most likely a short-range reconnaissance craft. A similar analysis of the four dead occupants was arranged by Dr. Bronk. It was the tentative conclusion of this group that although these creatures are human-like in appearance, the biological and evolutionary processes responsible for their development has apparently been quite different from those observed or postulated in Homo sapiens.

Numerous examples of what appear to be a form of writing were found . . . Efforts to decipher these have remained largely unsuccessful. (See Attachment' E") Equally unsuccessful have been efforts to determine the methods of propulsion or the nature or method of transmission of the power source involved. Research along these lines has been complicated by the complete absence of identifiable wings, propellers, jets or other conventional methods of propulsion and guidance, as well as a total lack of metallic wiring, vacuum tubes, or similar recognizable electronic components.[14]

Other corroborating evidence has been gathered. Glen Dennis was a graduate of San Francisco Mortuary College and lifelong resident of Roswell. On July 8, 1947, he received a call from the base and was asked "This is just a hypothetical situation . . . but do you have any three-foot-long, hermetically sealed caskets?" Dennis said they had one, and was asked how soon he could get more. He also responded to calls about embalming, embalming fluid, etc. Mr. Dennis later spoke to a nurse on the base who said she saw the bodies, that they were 3-4 feet tall, had four fingers, no thumbs, and that the anatomy of the arm was different from our own. When Dennis tried to call her later, he was told she was transferred to England. When he tried to write to her, he received letters stamped "addressee deceased." He heard she died in a plane crash.

Another researcher lists the following witnesses who corroborate the Roswell story:[15]

Table 4.1 Thirty-eight Witnesses to Various Aspects of the Roswell Incident

William Woody *	Mother Superior Bernadette *	Sister Capistrano*
Col. E. L. Pyles*	James Ragsdale*	Trudy Truelove*
Jason Ridgeway *	C. Curry Holdern ** ***	Dr. Bertrand Schultz ****
Maj. Jess Marcel **	Dr. Jess Marcel Jr. **	Col William Blanchard **
Maj Edwin Easley **	Sgt Thos. Gonzales ***	Steve Mac Kenzie ***
Lt Col Albert Duran ***	Warrant office Robt Thomas ****	Sgt Bill Rickett **
Sgt Melvin Brown ***	Frank Kaufmann **	W.O. Henderson ***

Sarah Holcomb ****	Helen Wachtet***	John Kronschroeder **
Maj Ellis Boldra **	Floyd Proctor**	William Proctor **
William Mac Brazel ** ****	Bill Brazel ** ****	Sallye Tadolini **
George Bush ***	County Sheriff Geo. Wilcox ****	Barbra Dugger ****
Frank Rove ****	Brig Gen Arthur Exon *** ****	

* witnessed the crash

** witnessed the debris

*** witnessed the bodies of the aliens

**** witness to the cover up.

Source of data: Jim Marrs. *Alien Agenda*. New York: Harper, 1997, pp 137-145. Note that Timothy Good in *Need to Know* (Pegasus Books, 2007) provides three additional witnesses to this incident, all with signed affidavits, whose names are not included above: Glenn Dennis, L.W. Maltais and Thomas DuBose [see pp 89-91].

After considerable study of this issue, billionaire Laurence Rockefeller urged President Clinton privately during a meeting in Jackson Hole, Wyoming, to investigate this story and release all essential records to the American people. Clinton said later, however,

> As far as I know, an alien spacecraft did not crash in Roswell, N.M. in 1947 . . . If the United States Air Force did recover alien bodies, they didn't tell me about it either, and I want to know.[16]

Philip Corso's Revelations[17]

In 1997 retired Lt. Col Philip Corso published "The day after Roswell." At the age of 82, he said he wanted to let the world know his secret, and that was that he not only viewed the body of an alien discovered at Roswell, but that he was in charge of the Roswell file in the Air Force in the early 1960s. His story is either a complete fraud or consummately breathtaking.

Corso says the alien craft likely was flying near Roswell because two top-secret bases existed there, White Sands, and the nuclear testing facility at Alamogordo. The craft had been tracked on radar for two days prior to crashing. It would appear at one corner of the radar screen and then dart across to another corner at seemingly impossible speeds.

It could change directions on a dime and reached speeds approaching 7,000 mph, and there were a few of them.

On the day of the crash a huge thunderstorm erupted and one craft appeared to have been struck by lightning and crashed as a consequence. When the wreckage was surrounded by Air Force personnel, four dark gray figures were found, one alive. The alien that was alive was breathing in a labored way and trying to crawl away from military personnel. When it failed to stop, they shot it.

No contact was made with the aliens, but the bodies are still preserved. Autopsies were performed at Walter Reed. The results showed that creature had a thin milky, lymphatic-like fluid rather than blood, a very slow metabolism, and possessed a huge heart and lungs. The heart had an internal diaphragm-like muscle that worked less hard and less often than the human heart muscle. Its organs decomposed far more rapidly than human organs.

The alien's bones were fibrous and thinner than comparable human bones. They also had lens-like goggles that let them see in darkness

Walter Reed Hospital doctors were fascinated by the inner skin: comprised of a thin layer of fatty tissue unlike any they'd ever seen before. And it was completely permeable, as if it were constantly exchanging chemicals back and forth with the combination blood/lymphatic system (p. 96).

Numerous artifacts were found on board.[18] Many years after the crash, Corso, on orders of his superior, General Arthur Trudeau, deliberately held the materials secret from the CIA and FBI. Recall that in 1947 Soviet intelligence had penetrated US security giving rise to their possession of the atomic bomb. This, in turn, spurred American paranoia as evidenced by the rise of Senator Joseph McCarthy. Since this was the single biggest secret in the United States, many layers of secrecy surrounded the Roswell discovery.

Corso's involvement was to direct the Air Force's office of "Foreign Technology." Operating his office as if artifacts had been purloined from foreign countries—instead of space aliens—his office directed research by various defense contractors into the nature of the objects. Patents were to be granted gratis to contractors who remained unaware as to their true origin.

Found onboard, for example, were many small gray wafers the size of quarters which seemed to have etchings. These, Corso alleges, ultimately led to development silicon chips. The aliens had a small pencil like device which emitted an invisible light ray that could cut through metal. Corso claims lasers were developed from the study of this object as well as particle beam weapons. He also asserts that night vision goggles, fiber optics, irradiated food, and supertenacity fibers evolved from research into Roswell artifacts.

Philip Corse Corso (right) receiving the bronze star in 1945

Within a year of publication, Corso passed away. Skeptics and debunkers swarmed like yellow jackets over his thesis.[19]

Dates, they said, had been distorted by Corso's faulty memory. His academic credentials were over-stated. The location of military bases and routes cited in the text were incorrect. Logical inconsistencies were pointed out, and there were humorous denials by defense contractors who allegedly came into possession of alien artifacts.

These seem to represent the most substantial rebuttals of Corso's work. However, what does appear to be true is that he was employed by the Air Force, that he worked under General Trudeau as stated, and that, indeed, he headed up the office of "Foreign Technology" in the Pentagon for a few years. Further, it appears to be true that he was affiliated with the National Security Council under Eisenhower as alleged. Attempts to corroborate his work are otherwise difficult.

Certainly one important endorsement came from Paul Hellyer, former Canadian Defense Minister, who told a Toronto audience that he "spoke to a retired Air Force General who confirmed the accuracy of the information in the book."[20]

On one radio interview a voice stress analysis was made of Corso and a second speaker. Neither showed evidence of lying.[21]

If his work is a colossal fraud—or a "complete fabrication"—as one blogger told this author, one wonders what motivation might exist for an eighty-two-year-old man to publish this kind of fairy tale thirty-four years after retiring from the Air Force.

What is of interest to this writer, a psychologist, is that he dedicated this alleged "complete fabrication" to the deceased and beloved General Trudeau under whom he proudly served his country. Again, one wonders what kind of psychopathology could propel an octogenarian to besmirch his Air Force career and compound the fraud by dedicating a book of lies to his dearest friend.

In an interview on this subject shortly before his death he said the following:

> The thing that I've done now is going to affect the future. That's why I bring the children in on it, the young ones. We're old now, we're going to be moving on. But they're going to be here. Let them know what happened. I think it's of great importance that those children are going to read this and know what happened and what it came from, and that it was true. It did happen. They have to know what's involved, and what it's leading to. They're the ones who will be involved in what it leads to. From that point of view, it's the most important thing I ever did.[22]

With Corso's text, we are placed at a fork in the road. Either this is a colossal fabrication perpetrated by a sinister octogenarian, or it is one of the most important pieces of literature to emerge from humankind. Corso's book unequivocally attests to the existence of a highly advanced alien civilization, which has interacted with our planet, our species left artifacts here, which are still in our possession.

As with so much of the data in this chapter, the decision on whether to accept Corso's detailed and articulate text or consider him a fraud is left to the reader.

Unusual Corroboration

Quite unrelated to Corso's text is a report by author Timothy Good, the author of *Need to Know: UFOs the Military and Intelligence*. Good spends most of his time in this book reviewing declassified military documents, but he reports a rather uncanny interview he had with Jean Kisling, a French pilot. Kisling had previously had an encounter with a UFO over Selfridge Field in Michigan in 1945. Good wanted to interview him about that episode since Kisling is alleged to have actually fired on that UFO, but in the course of their interview, a far more dramatic tale emerged:

> In the early 1950s Kisling, a commercial pilot, was flying the New York–Paris route. "One day when the crew arrived at Idelwild Airport," he began, "we were told that the regular schedule had been changed. The chief of security at the airport asked me to accompany him to his office. I was warned not to disclose the information he was about to reveal to me . . . He explained that this would now be a "special security" VIP flight to take a delegation of about twenty or thirty military officers from the Pentagon to Paris on a classified mission. Our Super Constellation had been parked away from the terminal with a military guard. We had a double or "heavy" crew on board. When I took my rest period during the flight across the Atlantic, I chatted to an elderly man with a beard. He revealed that he was a UFO specialist and that a very important unit in the Pentagon dealt exclusively with the subject. He said that a flying saucer had crashed at El Paso, Texas some time previously and that "small people" not from Earth had been recovered. I asked him why all this was kept secret. He replied that everyone would panic."[23]

The elderly gentleman on that flight likely was referring to the Roswell episode and the alleged recovery of alien bodies from the crash site.

Even in 2010, research and eyewitness testimony continues to flow. Recently a Roswell documentary revealed heretofore unknown aspects of this case:

- Few were aware that in 1947 Roswell was the location of the first nuclear air base, the Roswell Army Airfield. This was the home base of the Enola Gay, the plane that dropped the first atomic bomb on Hiroshima.

- Secondly, a week after the incident the government published a photo of General Ramey and Col Thomas Dubois holding foil from a weather balloon. The intent of the story was that the Roswell episode was a case of mistaken identity, and that all that was found was the remaining pieces of the weather balloon. Curiously, in the photo General Ramey is holding a crushed piece of paper in his hand. Using advanced computer techniques this paper has been deciphered in considerable detail and it appears to be a telegram, reading: SUB: ROSWELL. FWAAF ACKNOWELDGES THAT A DISK IS NEXT NEW FIND WEST OF THE CORDON. AT LOCATION WAS A WRECK NEAR OPERATION AT THE 'RANCH' AND THE VICTIMS. . . OF THE WRECK YOU FORWARDED TO THE ??? TEAM AT FORT WORTH, TEX. . . AVIATORS IN THE "DISC" THEY WILL SHIP FOR A1/8TH ARMYAMHC BY B20-ST OR C47.*†

- Col Dubois (in photo, p. 96) in his retirement said in a Youtube interview that the real debris from Roswell was never shown to the public. The interview may be accessed under the title "Brig Gen Thos Dubose admitting to government cover-up in Roswell in 1947." In addition, Dubois signed an affidavit in 1991 saying, "The material shown in the photographs taken in Maj. Gen. Ramey's office was a weather balloon. The weather balloon explanation for the material was a cover story to divert the attention of the press."‡ [Dubose was the highest-ranking military officer ever to have disclosed secret matters related to Roswell.]

- See photos on page 96.

---

* http://www.ufocasebook.com/rameymemo.html See also *The Roswell Crash: Startling new evidence.* DVD, Hosted by Bryant Gumbel.

† See also http://www.roswellproof.com/ If the reader wishes to see how this text was reconstructed from the crushed note in Gen Ramey's hand, go to http://roswellproof.com/Ramey_Message_lines_2009.rtf.

‡ http://www.roswellproof.com/dubose.html#anchor_3254

The Phoenix Lights

There are many UFO stories, indeed even some fascinating footage reported to show UFOs flying over Mexico City.[24] Finding stories with large numbers of corroborating witnesses, however, is a major problem. Our next selection of "best evidence" addresses this problem because it was an incident witnessed by over 700 individuals, photographs were taken, videos made, and even covered by CNN.[25]

Highlights follow:

In March, 1997 at 6:55 pm, a man in Henderson, Nevada witnessed a V-shaped object with six large lights on its leading edge . . . He described "a very strange cluster of distinctly red-orange lights, which consisted of 4–5 lights in the lead followed by a single light which appeared to be standing back from the others . . . . Within minutes, a barrage of phone calls came into the National UFO center, police, local news media, and nearby Luke Air Force Base about similar sightings. Three witnesses located just north of Phoenix reported seeing a huge V-shaped craft with five lights on its ventral service. The witnesses emphasized how gigantic the object was as it blocked out up to 70–90 degrees of the sky. Another group reported that the craft was approximately three kilometers wide, like a big black triangle. The object was first seen at close range over Phoenix between 8:30 and 8:45 PM. All in all "it made its presence known from the top of the Grand Canyon almost to the Mexican border."[26]

Its lights fell on streets that are 2.8 kilometers apart. Its flight path brought it to about 2,000 feet over the ground as estimated by witnesses leading various witnesses to estimate its length at between 900 feet, to 6000 feet. "Regardless of the type of formation seen, all observers agreed that the lights or objects were slow moving, very large, and totally silent."[27]

The transit across the region of observation lasted 106 minutes. For several minutes the city stood still as these lights swept overhead on their way toward Tucson, where truck drivers called one another on their CB radios, and families on the dark freeway stopped and stared in awe at the passing giant formation.[28]

A UFO organization has three videos of the sightings with time stamps showing the progression of the event across Arizona. Some individuals reported they saw silhouetted beings in the windows. Later the craft was seen by a family traveling from Tucson to Phoenix. One witness said "When it flew over us there was no noise, it was completely silent."[29]

"Phoenix Lights" appear over downtown

An intriguing eye-witness account comes from a physician:

I have been a psychiatrist for 22 years, board certified since 1984, and got my private pilot's license in 1985. I moved to Tucson from New Jersey in September 1991. I never observed anything in the sky that I could not explain until the night of March 13, 1997. We saw a row of approximately seven bright reddish-orange glowing orbs to the northwest at about 8:20-8:25pm just east of South Mountain and just west of Camelback Mountain. Then they moved over the west edge of the Gila Indian Reservation moving slowly south along I-10. In an instant, the lights were directly overhead. While our car was traveling at about 65 mph they seemed to hold directly overhead for about five to ten minutes, still holding formation at about 1,500 feet. With the moon roof open, we could hear no aircraft engine noise whatsoever. It was a diamond within a diamond pattern. I was impressed by the perfect symmetry of these lights. With a good deal of time to observe closely, these lights did not seem to be connected to anything ... From lead to trailer, the formation was about 300 yards across. There was no evidence of a flame, ionization, or smoke trail. The light itself did not seem to be illuminating either an attached physical craft or object on the ground. The lights formed no beams as a searchlight might. Altitude did not seem to change at all, and the formation slowly moved to the southeast toward Casa Grande."[30]

One witness said he saw three jets from nearby Luke Air force base try to intercept the UFO.

"As the jets approached the near objects, the objects shot straight up and disappeared, with the jets passing through the spot where the object had been hovering."[31] Although officials from Luke denied their aircraft had tracked the object, one truck driver observed three jets take off and veer right for the UFO.
I know those pilots saw it. Hell, I'll take a lie detector test on national TV if that guy from the base does the same thing. I wish the government would just admit it. You know what it's like in this city right now? It's like having 50,000 people in a stadium watch a football game and then having someone tell us we weren't there! [32]

Many photos were taken. Official explanations varied. The Air force said these were "flares" dropped by an Air force craft. However, most experts say flares emit smoke as they drop and they do not stay at a stationary altitude for such a long time as this craft did. A second debunker-theory was that this craft was a "stealth blimp" developed in the super secret Area 51 not far from Phoenix. An argument against such a theory, however, is that if the craft were super secret from Area 51, why would it be flying over metropolitan Phoenix and visible to so many?

Professional UFO-logists still consider the Phoenix Lights to represent not only a credible UFO event, but one of the most-well documented.[33]

Iceland, 1951

Another well-corroborated incident and considered part of our suite of best evidence occurred on Feb. 10, 1951. Lt. Graham Bethune, and his crew had an encounter with a UFO near Keflavik, Iceland.

240 miles out I saw something on the water 40 miles away. Moonset had occurred an hour previous. Nothing was scheduled to be in that area. I called it to the attention of my navigator and co-pilot. It looked like a city in the distance. There was a pattern to the lights on the water—an odd pattern. I thought it was a classified rescue mission. 20 miles out, the lights went out. A yellow halo appeared on the water. It flew towards us, some 20 miles, at approximately 1,000 miles per hour. It stopped 200 feet below us. I observed a faint dome shape to it. I had a knowing

that it was intelligently controlled—it came over to look at us. The object stayed about five miles away, at about a 45 degree angle. It flew with us, looking at us. I estimated its size at 300 feet in diameter. My plane had no guns. The on-board magnetic compass did spin. We had 31 passengers on board.

. . . We were interrogated in Iceland. It was obvious from the questions and demeanor of the US Navy men who debriefed us that they'd seen things out there before. A report on this event was kept at Wright-Patterson AFB. I found it in 1991 in the archives. I have the report along with letters from NICAP, Keyhoe's report to congress, and photos of the plane I was in. All five pilots described it, the UFO, the same—its size, the aura around it. A lieutenant who was on duty that night we were interrogated was told they traced it by radar in excess of 1,800 mph. No radar report was included in the 17-page report—it was missing from the report when I finally found it in 1991. Radar was confirmed at the time. I estimated the speed of the object at 1,000 mph. The other pilots estimated 1,000-1,500 mph. The fastest fighter we had at the time could go 500 mph. There were no jets at the time in February 1951.[34]

All five of the crew agreed with that they saw a UFO, and all five agreed on the facts as stated in the report. The UFO was observed for well over five minutes.

CSETI

The Center for the Study of Extraterrestrial Intelligence (CSETI) operates a UFO information network with a rapid mobilization investigative team which attempts to document UFO sightings with precision. Probably their most impressive work to date is a series of incidents which occurred on Santa Rosa Island in Florida. Using a 500,000 candle-power light, the organization first observed up to five UFOs, and then they tried to signal it.

To everyone's astonishment, when he flashed three times to the UFOs, the lead craft flashed back three times. Then after two flashes it returned a signal of two flashes, then five, and so on. There was a clear and definite congruence of the human-initiated signaling and the return signals of the craft . . . After several minutes of this activity, the UFOs "winked out" . . . The presence of over 50 credible witnesses, including two former Air Force pilots, five video tapes, two audio tapes, and a photographs establishes these events as a real and unequivocal . . . [35]

This report appears in Steven Greer's Extraterrestrial Contact with an appendix listing the 39 witnesses to this event.

Jim Marrs

A few years ago I completed work on a ten-year study of the assassination of John Fitzgerald Kennedy. *Conspiracy in Camelot: The Complete History of the Assassination of John Fitzgerald Kennedy* (Algora 2003) was intended as an academic, objective, and comprehensive treatment of the topic. In the course of my research, out of the 600-odd books written on JFK, three authors distinguished themselves to me as utterly objective, thorough to the extreme, rigidly scrupulous in the integrity of their research, and dispassionate in the character of their narrative: Anthony Summers, Jim Marrs, and Robert Grodin.

Strangely, when I was researching this UFO section of my book, I stumbled upon the name of Jim Marrs again and wondered what a skilled JFK researcher was doing writing a book called *Alien Agenda*! Out of acquired respect for Marrs, I bought the book and started into it only to discover the same meticulousness, thoroughness, and objectivity applied to such a far-out subject.

Although one of his chapters elicited a strong sense of disbelief, one aspect of his text deserves mention: the impression that the best evidence for the existence of UFOs is not the sightings themselves, but the serious effort of the government to suppress them. This is where Marrs developed some genuine skill from his work on the Kennedy assassination. Marrs, for example, uncovers a memo written by J. Edgar Hoover in the late 1940s to his second in command in the FBI and Hoover's lover and longtime companion, Clyde Tolson. The memo clearly shows that the army has come into possession of UFO debris which it held so secret that even the FBI couldn't get a look. From Hoover's scribbled reply to Tolson:

> I would do it but before agreeing to it we must insist upon full access to discs recovered. For instance in the [LA?] case the Army grabbed it and wouldn't let us have it for cursory examination.[36]

Most Americans heard of Project Blue Book, a government sponsored UFO inquiry whose conclusions were that evidence for UFOs was inconclusive at best. Marrs, however, uncovered many other secret UFO projects not intended for public perusal and many under the auspices of the CIA, e.g., Project Garnet, Project Gleem, Project Magnet, Project Moon Dust, Project POUNCE, Project Sign, Project SUNSTREAK, Project Bear, Project Aquarius.[37]

On March 22, 1950 another office memo to Hoover from the special agent in charge of the FBI's Washington office reports as follows:

> An investigator for the Air Force stated that three so-called flying saucers had been recovered in New Mexico. They were described as being circular in shape with raised centers, approximately 50 feet in diameter. Each one was occupied by three bodies of human shape, but only three feet tall, dressed in metallic cloth of a very fine texture. Each body was bandaged in a manner similar to the blackout suits used by speed fliers and test pilots."[38]

Marrs uncovers another telling incident which occurred in Bentwaters, England on Dec. 26–27, 1980. A large object was sighted, landed, investigating personnel saw it, reported and recorded it, and, as is usually the case, government skulking denied any official records existed about the event. Queries were dismissed as spurious, and the USAF denied any audiovisual recordings were ever made.

However, in 1983, following a Freedom of Information Act inquiry, an official report of the incident was indeed unearthed. The report is entitled "Unexplained Lights" dated Jan 13, 1981, written by a Colonel Halt and is quoted in its entirety.

1. Early in the morning of 27 Dec 80 (approximately 0300L), two USAF security police patrolmen saw unusual lights outside the back gate at RAF Woodbridge. Thinking an aircraft might have crashed or been forced down, they called for permission to go outside the gate to investigate . . . The individuals reported seeing a strange glowing object in the forest. The object was described as being metallic in appearance and triangular in shape, approximately two to three meters across the base and approximately two meters high. It illuminated the entire forest with a white light. The object itself had a pulsing red light on top and a bank(s) of blue lights underneath. The object was hovering or on legs. As the patrolmen approached the object, it maneuvered through the trees and disappeared. At this time the animals on a nearby farm went into a frenzy. The object was briefly sighted approximately an hour later near the back gate.

2. The next day, three depressions 1 1/2 feet deep and 7" in diameter were found where the object had been sighted on the ground. The following night (29 Dec. 80) the area was checked for radiation. Beta/Gamma readings of 0.12 milliroentgens were recorded with peak readings in the three depressions and near the center of the triangle formed by the depressions. A nearby tree had moderate .05-.07) readings on the side of the tree toward the depressions.

3. Later in the night a red sun-like light was seen through the trees. It moved about and pulsed. At one point it appeared to throw off glowing particles and then broke into five separate white objects and then disappeared. Immediately, thereafter, three star-like objects were noticed in the sky, two objects to the north and one to the south, all of which were about 10 degrees off the horizon. The objects moved rapidly in sharp angular movements and displayed red, green and blue lights. The objects to the north appeared to be elliptical through an 8-12 power lens. They then turned to full circles. The objects in the north remained in the sky for an hour or more. The object to the south was visible for two or three hours and beamed down a stream of light from time to time. Numerous individuals, including the undersigned witnessed the activities in paragraphs 2 and 3.[39]

When Col. Halt was later queried about this event, he said, "There are a lot of things that are not in my memo." Apparently one omission was that a film was made of these events, but the Air Force continued to deny the existence of any film. So in this case there are serious and believable witnesses, unusual radiation levels, and what appears to be an adamant and continuing effort by the government to suppress the information.

When one ruminates on the degree of secrecy around this kind of event, and compares the previously secret reports to the kinds of public denials made at the time, there is a ring of truth to this long legacy of sightings and rumors. However strenuous the efforts of the professional debunker community, the full story of the UFO phenomena does not appear to have been told. According or Marrs, "it is now obvious to any serious student of the subject that the U.S. government is hiding away information regarding UFOs and has been doing so for many years."[40]

Montana, March 16, 1967

There is an intriguing UFO story involving an incident in Montana in which two nuclear missile silos suddenly found all their electronics switched off for several hours. This was a strategic national security concern where 37-ton minuteman missiles were poised and ready to launch on command. Outside, a UFO was spotted, while inside the silo all the electronics for the missile command suddenly went dead for three hours. "There is no command in the capsule to turn the missile off. There is no switch—no off switch. They do not break. And I never saw an off alert missile in the three-and-a-half years I was a crewman,"[41] reports Lieutenant Col. Don Crawford. Twelve hours later that same day, another silo's electronics also went dead. Both silo commanders filed official, top-secret reports, but neither knew the other had experienced an identical incident, and neither commander was told what happened. Thirty years later, an independent investigator uncovered these two correlated national security breaches.[42]

Australia, 1978

Researcher Timothy Good provides solid evidence of a radio transmission between a pilot, Frederick Valentich, who vanished with his

Cessna 182 as he was en route from Melbourne to Tasmania. The incident is also described in other UFO texts. According to the transcript of the transmissions between Valentich and Melbourne Flight Service, he was being harassed by a large metallic object over the Bass Strait. He said, "It seems to be playing some sort of game with me. It's not an aircraft."[43] Then there was static. When his voice could be heard again, he said, "It is flying past. It has a long shape. Cannot identify more than that." There was another pause and then Valentich said, "It's coming for me right now." There was another pause and then he said, " . . . the thing is orbiting on top of me. It has a green light and sort of metallic light on the outside." His last words prior to his disappearance were " . . . ah, Melbourne, that strange aircraft is hovering on top of me again—it is hovering and it's not an aircraft." Valentich had a standard life jacket and radio beacon, but after an extensive search neither he nor the aircraft was ever found.

Soviet UFOs

In 1961 Yuri Gagarin became the first man in space, preceding John Glenn by a year. He died in a training flight in 1968. According to UFO sources, Gagarin said that, "UFOs are real, they fly at incredible speeds and that he would tell more about what he had seen in orbit, provided he be given permission to do so."[44]

Whether those remarks can genuinely be attributed to Gagarin is perhaps of less concern than the study of UFOs in the former Soviet Union. It reached its peak under former Premier Yuri Andropov. Andropov was the General Secretary of the Communist Party for some fifteen months in the early 1980s, but formerly the long-time chief of the KGB. He had a keen interest in the subject and launched a thirteen-year study of UFOs that enlisting some 4 million soldiers to monitor sightings.

Yuri Gagarin

Numerous documented cases came out of these investigations, including forty separate incidents where Soviet fighters engaged UFOs and one where three ground-to-air missiles were fired, all to no effect. It seems appropriate that we should include at least one Soviet UFO report as part of our suite of 'best evidence.' Here it is:

> That incident, which occurred on 4 October 1982 at an intercontinental ballistic missile (ICBM) silo at Byelokoroviche, Soviet Ukraine, brought the world to the brink of nuclear war. At around 18:00 soldiers and villagers saw a large, geometrically shaped object, apparently nearly 3,000 feet in diameter, hovering in the sky over the silo. Lieutenant Colonel Vladimir Plantonev, a missile engineer, described the UFO as having a completely even surface, with no visible portholes. Simultaneously, inside the missile silo, an emergency warning light indicated that a nuclear missile had switched to launch mode. "The communications officer said that somehow, something had entered the correct code" reported Knapp. But Moscow had not ordered a launch, nor had any personnel in the bunker touched the control panel. For fifteen agonizing seconds, technicians frantically scrambled to stop the launch. Then, without explanation, the launch sequence was aborted. No faults with the equipment were found by investigators . . . [45]

When debunker Jim Oberg got hold of this one, he had a few critical things to say. First, the actual Soviet report of the thirteen-year Andropov experiment yielded not even a "hint" of extraterrestrial involvement. As for the Ukrainian silo incident, (1) there was a record of parachute flares and night-bombing exercises occurring at another military base in "precisely that direction at precisely that time." (2) The missile base commander found it more convenient to blame extraterrestrials rather than his own maintenance teams for the scare of having the launch indicator lights malfunction.[46]

Negative Evidence

Sometimes the "best evidence" for UFOs comes from what you can't see. This next installment makes that observation abundantly clear.

Thanks to Citizens Against UFO Secrecy (CAUS), some UFO-related documents originating with the NSA were released in January 1980. The Agency admitted that many more were 'exempt from disclosure.' Later that year, NSA representative Eugene Yeates admitted in a court hearing that the NSA had found many documents on UFOs that were relevant to the FOIA request (Freedom of Information Act). Lawyer Peter Gersten, representing CAUS, under terms of the Freedom of Information Act (FOIA), filed suit against the NSA in the U.S. District Court, Washington DC to obtain 135 documents then admitted to being withheld by the Agency. After studying a twenty-one-page "above" Top Secret affidavit in camera, Judge Gesell ruled that the Agency was fully justified in withholding the documents in their entirety. The case was dismissed.[47]

It causes one to wonder if the conclusions of Project Blue Book and other government disclosures over the last few decades—namely that UFOs are not real nor of any genuine significance—what could Judge Gesell possibly have seen when he read that twenty-one page "above top secret" affidavit that prompted him to rule that those 135 UFO documents should be withheld in their entirety. Hmmm!

Authoritative Anecdotal Evidence

Up to this point we have concentrated upon the "best evidence" found in UFO literature, and naturally we have tried to avoid singular anecdotal accounts. However, some anecdotal testimony especially when it comes from highly reputable sources should be included. The USA's own NASA astronauts comprise our first foray into this area. For some of their commentary, see Table 4.2.

When we consider authoritative sources like these, there are problems that need to be looked at seriously: problems of corroboration, problems of important persons claiming they were misquoted, problems of taking comments out of context, and problems of hyperbole.

To take a step back for a moment: Probably the biggest question a human being might ask would be, "Is there life after death?" And the second most telling question could easily be "Have humans encountered alien civilizations now or in the past?" As these questions are of supreme importance, so should the data — and our reasoning — be as pristine as we can make it, so let us engage here in a bit of due diligence.

First, put the astronaut claims into perspective. Astronauts as a group are highly skilled. Their physical health and psychological stamina have been rigorously evaluated. Competition to become an astronaut is fierce. According to the president of the Kentucky Astronomical Society "You stand more of a chance to win a lottery than becoming an astronaut."[48]

So if we assume their honesty, integrity, and capacities to behave rationally under pressure are a few standard deviations above our own, when they say UFOs exist, or have followed them in space, we have to attach a certain gravitas to their commentary. They are obviously convincing. Who more deserves our trust?

Table 4.2 Astronaut Commentary on UFOs

Comment	Astronaut
In my official status, I cannot comment on ET contact. However, personally, I can assure you, we are not alone!	Charles J. Camarda (Ph.D.) NASA Astronaut
We all know that UFOs are real. All we need to ask is where do they come from, and what do they want.	Apollo 14 Astronaut Capt. Edgar Mitchell
All Apollo and Gemini flights were followed, both at a distance and sometimes also quite closely, by space vehicles of extraterrestrial origin - flying saucers, or UFOs, if you want to call them by that name. Every time it occurred, the astronauts informed Mission Control, who then ordered absolute silence.	Maurice Chatelain, former chief of NASA Communications Systems.
At no time, when the astronauts were in space were they alone there was a constant surveillance by UFOs	Scott Carpenter, NASA astronaut
At one stage we even thought it might be necessary to take evasive action to avoid a collision	Astronaut James McDivitt
I've been asked –about UFOs– and I've said publicly I thought they were somebody else, some other civilization.	Astronaut Eugene Cernan, Apollo 17, in Los Angeles Times, 1973

Other NASA astronauts who have reported UFO sightings are: Major Gordon Cooper Donald Slayton, Major Robert White, Joseph A. Walker, Ed White, James Lovell, Frank Borman, Neil Armstrong, John Glenn and Edwin Aldrin (Source: http://www.syti.net/UFOSightings.html)	

Case closed? Not so fast! Time to hear from the skeptics and de-bunkers. Probably the most prestigious are Michael Shermer, publisher of *Skeptic Magazine,* and James Olberg. Mr. Olberg in particular is to be applauded for his scholarship. Here is a table summarizing the work of Olberg and others as they analyzed NASA astronaut expert testimony on the presence of UFOs:

Table 4.3 Debunker Arguments on Astronaut Sources

NASA Astronaut	Skeptic claims	Is skeptic likely to be accurate?
Scott Carpenter	No reliable source for story; uncorroborated	Yes
Joe Walker	Story uncorroborated; complete fabrication	Yes
James McDivitt	Comments distorted and exaggerated by UFO enthusiasts	No
James Lovell	Misquoted	Yes
Buzz Aldrin	Comments distorted	Yes
Frank Borman	Fictitious quote	Yes
John Glenn	Quote taken out of context and exaggerated	Yes
Neil Armstrong	Never corroborated by Armstrong	Yes
Maurice Chatelain	Only worked as NASA subcontractor; never chief of NASA communications	Yes

Sources: Astronaut UFO sightings, James Oberg, Skeptical Inquirer, Vol III, 1978; see also http://www.ufologie.net/htm/astronauts.htm; see also http://members.shaw.ca/mjfinley/gilbert.html

So when astronaut "expert witness" testimony is put through a skeptic's filter, it loses much of its luster. Of nine astronaut reports scrutinized, eight fail—at least from this writer's point of view.

In UFO literature Neil Armstrong allegedly sent a secret transmission from the moon regarding a huge UFO, and that quote circulates round the internet faster than light:

> These babies were huge, sir! Enormous! Oh, God! You wouldn't believe it! . . . I'm telling you there are other space-craft out there . . . lined up on the far side of the crater edge! . . . They're on the moon watching us! [49]

Did Neil Armstrong really say that? Can we corroborate that quotation? Armstrong went into virtual seclusion since his moon walk and never spoke about this UFO issue, ever. When Buzz Aldrin is asked about it, he says politely that he will let Neil Armstrong speak for himself. Some argue one day Armstrong may break his silence; others say it just simply never happened.

So we are left with enthusiastic UFO buffs who proliferate misquotes or fictitious quotes of astronauts and leave us scratching our heads.

At the same time all of their comments cannot be dismissed either. Many astronauts indeed have corroborated sightings, and their comments are fully available on Youtube. Here is a table listing videos quoting astronaut and cosmonaut sources directly and in their own words:

Table 4.4 Video Testimonies of NASA Astronauts Reporting UFOs.

Astronaut	Title of Youtube video
James McDivitt	"UFOs are real, 1979"
Edgar Mitchell	"Edgar Mitchell Interview"
Gordon Cooper	"Gordon Cooper talks about UFOs"
Victor Afanasyev (Cosmonaut)	"Sightings Russian cosmonaut UFO sightings"

In addition to these video sources, return for a moment to the Bentwater's episode. To recapitulate, the deputy base commander, Col. Halt, reported the series of UFO incidents which happened over a few days near his Air Force base in England. He described the events in a report he filed and forwarded to his superiors along with video footage. The government later said that no UFO happened in this location, no report existed, none was forwarded by Col. Halt, and there was no video footage. Three years later, however, Freedom of Information Act disclosures revealed all of that was untrue. Not only was there a report, but, since retiring, Col Halt came forward to verify that the incidents indeed occurred and that a video was made. (Halt's Youtube account may be found located under an Italian title: "UFO Testimonianza ex col. C. Halt ita sottotitoli".)

More Problems with Corroboration

While you may take some solace in finding video testimony of astronauts themselves, there still exists the phenomenon of UFO community buzzing with rumors, innuendo, and wittingly or unwittingly spreading false information in its zeal and enthusiasm.

In my own attempts at verification, I felt that if former President of the USSR, Michael Gorbachev, or a James Woolsey, the retired director of the CIA, or President Harry Truman actually said UFOs were real, these people were certainly in a position to know and therefore their commentary, if corroborated, surely represented some of the best evidence anyone could offer to answer the fundamental question posed by this book: have aliens been in contact with humanity?

But my attempts were disappointing to the extreme: I wrote to Margaret Truman through the Truman Presidential Library to ask if her father uttered the words, "I can assure you that flying saucers, given that they exist, are not constructed by any power on earth." Supposedly he delivered them in an impromptu press conference in Key West in 1950, but debunkers say Truman was in Key West then and never said that. Margaret Truman's secretary politely replied that Ms. Truman did not comment on such matters.

James Woolsey failed to reply to my query, and, as for Mr. Gorbachev, a letter translated into Russian and sent to the Gorbachev Foundation went ignored. From these attempts we should probably realize that evidence, quotations, and testimony regarding our important question really may not be as pristine, untainted, or unambiguous as we might otherwise hope.

Now if we strip out comments by astronauts, and dip into the scientific community, we seem to bang right into the same schizophrenic wall. Here are more "authoritative voices" either adding to or subtracting from the evidence we are trying to accumulate.

Adding More to the Confusion

Table 4.5 Scientific Voices on UFOs

Pro	Con
"The least improbable explanation is that these things are artificial and controlled . . . my opinion for some time has been that they have an extraterrestrial origin." —Dr. Maurice Biot, Aerodynamicist and Mathematical Physicist	"I do not think the evidence is at all persuasive, that UFOs are of intelligent extraterrestrial origin." —Carl Sagan, Astronomer, Harvard, Cornell
"I was forced to conclude that there is a great likelihood that Earth is being visited by highly advanced aerospace vehicles under highly 'intelligent' control indeed." —Dr. Richard F. Haines, retired NASA senior research scientist at Ames Research Center and the Research Institute for Advanced Computer Science	Yes, because I personally don't think they are here . . . If aliens have been visiting the Earth for 50 years, you would think that it would not be so hard to convince a lot of people that that was true. It's convinced 50 percent of the American public, but it's convinced very few academics. —Seth Shostak, Ph.D., Princeton Astronomer & Director SETI institute
"I have absolutely no idea where the UFOs come from or how they are operated, but after ten years of research, I know they are something from outside our atmosphere." —Dr. James E. McDonald, Professor of Atmospheric Physics, University of Arizona.	"I am discounting reports of UFOs. If there is a government conspiracy to suppress the reports and keep for itself the scientific knowledge the aliens bring, it seems to have been a singularly ineffective policy so far. Furthermore, despite an extensive search by the SETI project, we haven't heard any alien television quiz shows. This probably indicates that there are no alien civilizations at our stage of development within the radius of a few hundred light years." —Stephen Hawking, Theoretical Physicist

Sources: Interview with Phillip Klaas. http://www.pbs.org/wgbh/nova/aliens/
philipklass.html; see also source: http://www.ufoevidence.org/documents/
doc1744.htm; additional sources for Carl Sagan are: http://www.ncas.org/ufo-
symposium/sagan.html; for Shoshtak see http://www.space.com/sciencefiction/
phenomena/ufo_seti_000619.html

For Hawking see: http://woodside.blogs.com/cosmologycuriosity/2008/06/ste-
phen-hawking.html

Nobel laureate physicist Frank Wilczek says, "There is no sign of intelligent life," and physics professor John Kasher believes exactly the opposite.[50] Go figure!

Sources of Evidence in the Digital Age

We live in era where the average person is carrying a cell phone, and thousands walk around with video cameras. The explosion of UFO snapshots and video clips is enormous. At the same time the software for editing video can be found on just about any desktop computer, so we can assume two things: sightings will increase and so will hoaxes.

A cursory trip through *Youtube* reveals find absolutely dramatic footage of what are called UFOs, which leave one breathless and wondering, "Is this real or am I watching a well-crafted fake?"

Two examples are listed below.

Youtube video title	URL
CGI UFO fleet Mexico	http://www.youtube.com/watch?v=v5FOp8CMJtk
Amazingly clear UFO	http://www.youtube.com/watch?v=6ApAJjK96zc

* Youtube videos can be accessed by searching under the title only.

Going to the Source

Obviously, the official line has been to pooh-pooh the subject, but some curious voices have whispered from the shadows with commentary that makes one sit up and take notice, one even from President Clinton's White House Chief of Staff, John Podesta.

The following table presents a short list those comments:

Table 4.6. Curious Comments by Insiders

Official	Statements
John Podesta, Chief of Staff under President Clinton	It's time to open the books. . . on the question of government investigations of UFOs. We ought to do it because the American people, quite frankly, can handle the truth; and we ought to do it because it's the law. (1)
Col. Joseph J. Bryan, Psychological Operations, CIA	I am aware that hundreds of military and airline pilots, airport personnel, astronomers, missile trackers, and other competent observers have reported sightings of Unidentified Flying Objects . . . It is my opinion that the UFO devices are under intelligent control...(2)
Vice Admiral Roscoe Hillenkoetter, Former director of the CIA (1947-50)	It is time for the truth to be brought out in open Congressional hearings. Behind the scenes high ranking Air Force officers are soberly concerned about the UFOs, but through official secrecy and ridicule, many citizens are led to believe the unknown flying objects are nonsense. (3)
General Hoyt S. Vanderberg, Chief of Staff, US. Air Force,	Subject: Destruction of Air Intelligence Report Number 100-203-79: It is requested that action be taken to destroy all copies of Top Secret Air Intelligence Report Number 100-203-79, subject "Analysis of Flying Object Accidents in the U.S. dated Dec, 1948." (4)
Robert Crowley, Director of Operations, CIA (1986)	"UFOs are the most sensitive subject in the intelligence community." (5)
Paul Hellyer, Canadian Minister of Defense Minister (1963-67) Deputy Prime Minister under Pierre Trudeau	"UFOs are as real as the airplanes that fly over your head." (Sept, 25, 2005)
Lord Hill-Norton, Chief of the Defence Staff (UK) and Chairman of the NATO Military Committee.	"The evidence is now so consistent and so overwhelming that no reasonably intelligent person can deny that something unexplained is going on in our atmosphere." (7)

L. Clerebaut, Secretary General, Belgian Government in charge of investigating UFO sightings	"Scientifically we eliminate the simple hypotheses: It's not a plane. It's not a helicopter. It's not a natural phenomenon because the descriptions don't match. Therefore this global phenomenon resists any other explanation. The only remaining hypothesis is the hypothesis of extraterrestrial origin." (8)

(1) Norman, Tony (2 December 2008). "Change is coming (but not for space aliens)". *Pittsburgh Post-Gazette*. Also Timothy Good, Ibid., p. 308.

(2) Frank Edwards, *Flying Saucers, Here and Now!* Lyle Stuart publisher, New York, 1967, p. 42-43

(3) Major Donald Keyhoe, *Aliens From Space? The real story of Unidentified Flying Objects*: Panther, St. Albans, UK, 1975, pp 102-103

(4) *National Archives* Cited in Timothy Good, Ibid., p. 114.

(5) Terry Hansen, *The Missing Times: News Media Complicity in the UFO Cover-up*, Xlibris Corp, 2000, p. 299

(6) "Paul Hellyer Speaks" *UFO Magazine*, Vol 20, 2006, p. 36-39.

(7) Foreword to *Beyond Top Secret*.

(8) http://www.kellymoore.net/U_F_O_Roswell_New_Mexico.html

Before you become too confident that insiders have admitted UFOs are real and it's okay to jump onto the bandwagon of believers, disciples, and devotees, along comes another story, this time from the BBC, that might just curb that enthusiasm. A confidential Ministry of Defense report in England—actually a top secret report pried open through a Freedom of Information lawsuit—surprised everybody. Instead of some hush-hush for-your-eyes only white paper about UFOs and their existence, it came to exactly the opposite conclusion. The secret, four-hundred page report said, "No evidence exists to suggest that the phenomena seen are hostile or under any type of control, other than that of natural physical forces."[51] Elegant disinformation, perhaps, or maybe we're back to square one.

Conclusion

In the UFO arena we are limited to anecdotal data (the Buzz Aldrin quote is from "Apollo 11 say UFO" http://ufos.about.com/b/2006/07/31/apollo-11-saw-ufo.htm), a fair number of video recordings that may or may not have been doctored, occasionally released secret reports, and conflicting scientific and astronaut testimony; from that, an intelligent researcher must formulate the most rational decision he or she can, on one of the most pregnant and telling questions facing humanity.

A study published in the *Journal of Abnormal Psychology* (1993) showed that individuals who believed in or reported UFOs—even UFO abductions—did not show any higher incidence of psychological disturbance than those who did not. So you can take some solace that whatever you decide, you're not likely mentally ill merely because of your opinions on this subject.[52]

I'll conclude this chapter with one story that moved me personally, despite the fact that it suffers from all the problems of corroboration that other reports do. It certainly does not rank as part of the "best evidence" we were attempting to collate in this chapter—it is, nonetheless, moving and actually involves the extremely rare event of a person losing his life because of a UFO.

In January, 1948 Kentucky Air National Guard Captain Thomas F. Mantell was piloting an F-051 (a postwar version of the P-51 Mustang). Citizens were reporting a large circular object over Mansville, Kentucky. Mantell was asked to fly to the area to investigate. He and two other pilots began climbing in an effort to intercept the UFO. They soon reached fifteen thousand feet . . . Mantell radioed:

> The object is direct ahead of and above me now, moving at about half my speed. It appears to be a metallic object or possibly reflection of sun from a metallic object and it is of tremendous size. I'm still climbing. I'm trying to close in for a better look.[53]

Planes did not reach 20,000 feet easily in those days and Mantell's two companions turned their World War II fighters back. Mantell, however, kept going, reaching 30,000 feet, whereupon he passed out from lack of oxygen. His plane went into a spiral dive and crashed, killing him. He had been in constant contact with his radio control tower, however, and his last words before he perished were . . . "My God, I see people in this thing!"[54]

*The April 25, 1988, issue of The New Yorker carried an inter-
view with retired Air Force Reserve Major General and former U.S.
Senator from Arizona, Barry Goldwater, who said he repeatedly asked
his friend General LeMay if he (Goldwater) might have access to the
secret "Blue Room" at Wright Patterson Air Force Base, alleged ... to
contain UFO evidence. According to Goldwater, an angry LeMay gave
him "holy hell" and said, "Not only can't you get into it, but don't you
ever mention it to me again!*[55]

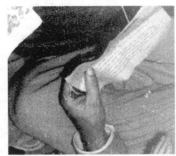

Photos are referenced on page 75.

Endnotes

1 Steven Greer, *Extraterrestrial Contact: The Evidence and Implications*. Afton, VA: Crossing Point, 1999 p.xvii.

2 Truman, Harry. White House Press conference, April 4, 1950; cited in Greer, *Ibid.*, p. 110. This quotation has been challenged, alleging that Truman was in Key West at the time, not Washington.

3 The source of Mr. Gorbachev's remarks is difficult to determine. One internet source, http://www.ufologie.net/htm/quotes.htm, reports that, "Former USSR leader Mikhail Gorbachev gave this reply to workers in the Urals. *Soviet Youth* magazine, May 4, 1990, reported in CIA declassified FBIS." This is the closest this author was able to get to the origin of the quotation. It is repeated frequently on the internet and in UFO circles.

4 http://www.spacequotations.com/ufoquotes.html

5 *Shadows over the Stars*, cited in Peter Kolosimo, *Ibid.*, p. 66.

6 Jim Marrs, *Alien Agenda*, New York: Harper Collins, 1997.

7 Cited in Peter Kolosimo, *Ibid.*, p. 74.

8 Debunkers alleged that this piece was written by a "stringer" named Hayden who had written other satirical pieces. They say Judge Proctor had no windmill and the story was a hoax. However, as there was no radio in those days, it was curious that in a five-day period between April 15 and April 19, over 21 different towns in Texas reported sightings of an unusual flying airship. See Jim Marrs, *Ibid.*, ppxxix

9 Peter Kolosimo, *Not of this world, Ibid.*, p. 83.

10 Greer, *Ibid.*, p. 21, p. 28.

11 Some important books on this subject are Saler, B., Ziegler, C. & Moore, C. *UFO Crash at Roswell: the The Genesis of a Modern Myth*: Washington: Smithsonian Institution Press, 1997; Corse, P. *The Day after Roswell*, Pocket Books, 1997; McAndrew, J., *The Roswell Report: Case Closed*. Washington: U.S. Government Printing Office, 1997.

12 Source: http://www.thewhyfiles.co.uk/images/rospaper.jpg

13 Glenn Dennis is active in the UFO Museum and Research Center in Roswell. Source of Dennis' commentary is John H. Sime "Embalming E.T." *Funerals of the Famous II*, New Jersey: Kates-Boylston Publishers, Vol. 2. 1996, pp. 30-34

14 Source: http://www.v-j-enterprises.com/mjl2.html

15 Jim Marrs. *Alien Agenda*. New York: Harper, 1997, pp 137-145

16 http://www.v-j-enterprises.com/dvettrk.html. There are other curious facts about Roswell too. It was a location where the United States was beginning to test missiles in their earliest developmental stages. Secondly, it was located very close to the 509th bomb group, the only squadron in the world which packed a military arsenal of atomic weapons. See Lynne Kitei: *The Phoenix Lights. Ibid.*, p. 113

17 Philip Corso *The Day after Roswell*. New York, Pocket Books, 1997.

18 One of the materials discovered was a dull gray metallic cloth-like material that seemed to shine up from the sand. The officer at the wreckage "stuffed it into his fist and rolled it into a ball. Then he released it and the metallic fabric snapped back into shape without any creases or folds. . . . When I tried to cut it with scissors the arms just slid right off without making even a nick in the fibers. If you tried to stretch it, it bounced back" (p.4). However preposterous this may sound to the reader, in 1964 prior to receiving any advanced degrees, I was teaching fourth grade outside of Ann Arbor Michigan, where the University of Michigan is located. One of my students, whose father worked in a research facility, brought me a small piece of material, exactly as Corso describes. I played with this metallic cloth, which was probably the thickness of aluminum foil. It had precisely these properties. I could not cut it with scissors, could not puncture it with a pencil, pen, or protractor, and it bounced back to its creaseless state after crushing. I was amazed.

19 One more respected skeptic is Stanton Friedman, whose paper is worth review. See http://www.v-j-enterprises.com/sfcorso.html

20 http://www.absoluteastronomy.com/topics/Paul_Hellyer

21 http://www.ufomind.com/people/c/corso/

22 http://www.geocities.com/Area51/shadowlands/6583/roswell018.html

23 Timothy Good. *Need to Know*. New York: Pegasus Books, 2007, p. 177.

24 The reader is invited to review streaming video off the internet showing the best footage of UFOs available including footage taken by an American astronaut near the moon: "http://bjbooth.topcities.com/Video/cropcircle.ram

25 The CNN footage of the Phoenix Lights can be seen on youtube under the title: "real UFO sighting during CNN broadcast"

26 Lynne Kitei, *The Phoenix Lights*, Charlottesville, VA: Hampton Roads Publishing, 2000, p.xiii.

27 Greet, *Ibid.*, p. 164.

28 Kitei, *Ibid.*, p. 2.

29 Kitei, *Ibid.*, p. 16.

30 Kitei, *Ibid.*, pp 132-133. Many of the sources in this section come from Lynne Kitei's The Phoenix Lights. Dr. Kitei is an MD in Phoenix and lives in a home with an expansive view of the Phoenix area. Never having been interested in UFOs she saw the Phoenix lights on more than one occasion and photographed them, even videotaping them. The photo which appears in this section was courtesy of Dr. Kitei as well. Fearing that her medical reputation could be injured by appearing as a UFO observer, for a long time she was interviewed by the media only as "Dr. X". Finally, she came forward to write a book about the subject because it had become so important, and her prior Dr. X appellation was discarded.

31 Kitei, *Ibid.*, p. 20.

32 Kitei, *Ibid.* p.55. A curious anecdote is that former Governor Fife Symington, 10 years after the event, admitted that he made fun of the UFO encounter at the time in order not to cause a panic. He now says that he too saw the lights and believed they were extraterrestrial. Source: "Arizona: O.K., it was a UFO." *New York Times*, March 24, 2007, p. A10.

33 Source: http://www.gpgwebdesign.com.au/latest.phoenix230302.htm

34 Greer, *Ibid.*, pp. 127-128.

35 Greer, *Ibid.* pp 204-205.

36 Researchers believe the reference to LA in this memo referred to Los Alamos where the debris from the Roswell incident may have been taken. Quotation cited in Jim Marrs, *Alien Agenda*, New York, Harper, 1997, p. 180.

37 Jim Marrs, *Alien Agenda*. New York: Harper Collins, 1997. Kitei reports another secret study group called Operation Blue Fly. See Kitei, *Ibid.*, p. 126

38 *Ibid.*

39 Jim Marrs, *Ibid.*, pp 244-246.

40 Jim Marrs, *Ibid.*, p. 248.

41 Kitei, *Ibid.*, p. 118.

42 Kitei, *Ibid.*, p. 118.

43 Timothy Good, *Ibid.*, p. 309-310; See transcript of radio transmission, p. 318. See also Rupert Matthews, *Alien Encounters*, New Jersey, Chartwell Books, 2008, p. 66.

44 http://ufoweek.com/2009/06/03/soviet-ufos-on-the-history-channel/

45 Cited in Timothy Good, 2009, pp 351-352.

46 Jim Oberg, Russian UFO Research Revealed. http://www.rense.com/general3/rusufo.htm

47 Timothy Good, *Ibid.*, p. 338.

48 Source: http://answers.yahoo.com/question/index?qid=20090820122627AAxK5ug

49 http://www.abovetopsecret.com/forum/thread447131/pg1

50 For Frank Wilczek, Science News, June 20, 2009, p. 4. Patricia Ross interview, Feb. 24, 2009, Examiner.com: source; http://www.examiner.com/x-2925-Omaha-Paranormal-Examiner-y2009m2d24-Top-physicist-believes-that-UFOs-are-realAnd-that-they-have-visited-us

51 Mark Simpson, BBC News, "UFO study finds no signs of aliens," May 7, 2006. See http://news.bbc.co.uk/2/hi/uk_news/4981720.stm

52 Cited in *Newsweek*: http://www.newsweek.com/id/96014/page/3

53 Jim Marrs, *Ibid.*, p. 154.

54 Jim Marrs, *Ibid.*, p. 154.

55 Quote appears genuine. It may also be found in the following sources: http://en.wikipedia.org/wiki/Curtis_LeMay ; see also http://kevinrandle.blogspot.com/2008/05/barry-goldwater-and-curtis-lemay.html as well as http://www.unexplainable.net/artman/publish/article_2449.shtml. Interviewed on Larry King, Senator Goldwater also mentioned Wright-Patterson and undisclosed UFO evidence.

5. PARANORMAL EVIDENCE FOR EXTRATERRESTRIAL CONTACT: CROP CIRCLES

The most beautiful thing we can experience is the mysterious.
It is the source of all true art and all science. He to whom
this emotion is a stranger, who can no longer
pause to wonder and stand rapt in awe, is
as good as dead: his eyes are closed.
—Albert Einstein

Another branch on our paranormal journey is the strange phenomenon of crop circles. They first appeared in 1678.

A drawing of a crop circle in 1678 is described as follows:

Being a True relation of a Farmer, who Bargaining with a Poor Mower, about the Cutting down of Three Half Acres of Oats: upon the Mower's asking too much, the Farmer swore That the Devil should Mow it rather than He. And so it fell out, that very Night, the Crop of Aot shew'd as if it had been all of a Flame: but the next Morning appear'd so neatly mow'd by the Devil or some Infernal Spirit, that no Mortal Man was able to do the like. Also, How the said Oats ly now in the field, and the Owner has not Power to fetch them away. Licensed August 22, 1678 [1]

These strange figures in recent times have been found in England, Germany, France, Spain, Bulgaria, Israel, Canada, Russia, Japan, China and New Zealand. Many are probable hoaxes perpetrated by individuals for whatever reasons. Some are admitted; many others aren't.

A survey shows that 50 percent of Americans believe crop circles are hoaxes. As these mysterious figures have moved from tabloids into peer-reviewed scientific journals, however, a number of peculiarities have emerged which suggest not all are as easily explained away. Here, we would like to review some of that evidence.

Despite the discovery of over ten-thousand circles, only about 70 individuals have actually been seen, or caught, making them.[2]

Most other eye-witness accounts are like UFO reports and allege that "BOLs" (balls of light) appear and carve them into fields. Certainly if ten thousand crop circles were constructed—and all were sculpted by dexterous vandals— it is curious that only 70 incidents were observed while 9,730 stealthy hoaxers are grinning ear-to-ear in their anonymity. On the stealth scale, that is an extremely high score.

In Sonoma, California a mathematically sophisticated crop circle appeared. Four high school students boasted they were bored and fessed up to making it, with all the attendant braggadocio for their age. However, when a group of physicists noticed the geometry was far beyond anything taught in high school mathematics, they interviewed the hoaxers and found none able to reproduce the figure on paper. The hoaxers themselves were a hoax![3]

In another case, three MIT undergraduates attempted to replicate a crop circle, and their efforts were anything but stunning. (View it at http://www.bltresearch.com/published/mit.php.)

One curious investigator said, when walking through a complex and intriguing crop circle, "In just moments it became only too clear how difficult it would have been to have constructed such a unique pattern in the tall standing wheat. Being completely flat made it impossible to see where you were in the design, which I estimated to be over 60 yards in length and breadth . . . If it was a hoax, well, then these people were certainly not messing about." [4]

Stonehenge Crop Circle, 1996

One of the most awe inspiring circles ever created appeared in Stonehenge in 1996. This formation is a very short distance from Stonehenge itself, less than a mile, and it comprises 151 circles which cover an area of over 380 feet. It appears to have been created in broad daylight:

> A pilot, Graham Taylor, had flown over Stonehenge at about 5:30 p.m., and had not seen anything, yet a little more than half an hour later, he flew back and discovered the magnificent formation. "My friend has been looking at crop circles with me since 1988, and he knows what he is looking for. He flew over there at half past five in the afternoon, and he flew around Stonehenge seven times. The crop circles weren't there at half past five." David Kinston, ex-RAF pilot and now full time crop circle researcher, told me that three independent witnesses had been found, all confirming the same event: *the 1996 Stonehenge formation appeared within about half an hour during broad daylight.* A farm worker also confirmed the absence of any shape in the field throughout the day, and a Stonehenge security guard confirmed that there was nothing unusual there all day long. [5]

A huge traffic jam at Stonehenge occurred that day as spectators rushed to see the new crop circle created right under their noses. As one researcher put it, "Was it possible that a group of human beings, skilled in both advanced mathematics and environmental art, had mastered the principle of invisibility and flouted the laws of gravity to levitate above the untouched wheat in order to create this masterpiece?" [6]

Another circle appeared in the form of a double helix in a wheat field in the English village of Alton Barnes in Wiltshire and this delicate design was made in less than a four-hour span of time.[7]

More on Hoaxes

Crop circle hoaxers usually walk on boards using simple hand or foot stomping methods. The method used by self-proclaimed British hoaxers Doug Bower and Dave Chorley involved garden rollers or rotating PVC pipes. But as these figures have received closer scrutiny, a number of anomalies have been recorded which challenge calling all crop circles fakes.

Most hoaxes are made in grain fields, but rarely in maize, carrots, potatoes, mustard, spinach, tobacco, grass, snow, or other milieux where the circles also have been found. When one investigator looked at a crop circle made in a carrot patch, his footprint was immediately noted some 5 cm. deep, and yet within the patch, not a single footprint was visible. Secondly, burn marks were observed on the plants inside the circle, some burned to ashes, and sometimes the entire leaf had been burned away, yet no similar marks were seen on the plants outside the circle.[8]

> Unusual deposits have been found inside crop circles, magnesium oxide [magnetic iron ore]. "American researchers measured the magnetite concentration in the soil inside numerous crop circles all around the world. The macroscopic appearance of crop circle magnetite has been recognized as meteoritic in origin. This meteoritic dust drifts down daily from the atmosphere on earth resulting in a nominal maximum concentration of 0.4mg per gram of soil. Any higher concentration is remarkable. In crop circles, nevertheless, concentrations of 20 to even 250 mg per gram of soil have been found, which is more than a six hundredfold increase of the normal value."[9]

Dutch researchers identified scores of dead flies stuck on the seed heads of wheat plants inside a crop circle. The insects were firmly stuck with their tongues against the ears and their legs and wings spread out widely as in a spasm. Pesticides could be excluded. Some of the flies had literally exploded: their legs, pieces of their bodies and wings, and their heads were scattered over the seed heads. Other flies however were still in a perfect state, and looked as if they could fly away at any moment. Closer inspection showed they were dead.[10]

Germination anomalies have been noted where in a mature crop, the seeds seemed to be energized so that they grew at up to five times the normal rate. Some equipment near crop circles shows unusual burn marks. Cellular anomalies, the structured lengthening of the nodes in corn plants, exploded nodes, and even unnatural radioactivity have also been observed inside the formation.

Marshall Dudley and Michael Chorost recently published a report showing the discovery of thirteen short-lived radionuclides [radioactive isotopes] in soil samples taken from an English crop circle, including tellurium-199m, lead-203, and rhodium-102 with a natural lifetime of days only. The isotopes were found in two soil samples taken within the crop circles and were absent in a control sample taken ten meters outside the formation.[11] "The presence of these particular short-lived radionuclides is surprising, since they must be synthesized in particle accelerators or experimental nuclear reactors which makes them very difficult and expensive to obtain."[12]

Infrared photographs of known hoaxes compared to circles thought to be genuine (or unadmitted by hoaxers) reveal a visible heat signature not found with admitted hoaxes.[13]

Mathematical Studies of Crop Circles

One of the first peer-reviewed studies published on crop circles came from the former chairman of the astronomy department at Boston University, Dr. Gerald Hawkins. Analyzing dozens of photographs in which proportions, circle diameters, and the areas inside the rings were known, Hawkins discovered that ratios showed that they corresponded to integer numbers, more specifically diatonic ratios, similar to the distance between the white keys of a piano keyboard. All the *known* hoaxes Hawkins reviewed did *not possess this characteristic*, but the others did.[14]

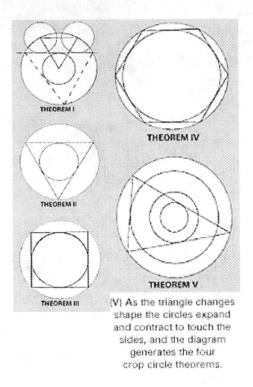

THEOREM I

THEOREM IV

THEOREM II

THEOREM V

THEOREM III

[V] As the triangle changes shape the circles expand and contract to touch the sides, and the diagram generates the four crop circle theorems.

In a second study Hawkins showed that numerous pictographs possessed five geometric theorems (shown above) deeply embedded within their structures.[15]

Euclid's Undiscovered Theorem Appears

Hawkins was a distinguished radio astronomer associated with Jodrell Bank, and the first to discover that Stonehenge may have been a calendar measuring the rising and setting of the sun and moon over an 18.6 year cycle.

Here are excerpts of a 1992 interview he gave about crop circles:

> When asked how he got interested, Hawkins said he was intrigued by a book entitled *Circular Evidence*. He measured patterns in the circles and found incredible, tell-tale ratios. "The ratios I found, such as 3/2, 5/4, 9/8, 'rang a bell' in my head because they are the numbers which musicologists call the 'perfect' intervals

of the major scale . . . I took every pattern in their book, *Circular Evidence*. I found that some of them were listed as accurately measured and some were listed as roughly or approximately measured . . . We finished up with 19 accurately measured formations, of which 12 were major diatonic . . . The difficulty of hitting a diatonic ratio just by chance is enormous."

When asked if he felt these formations could be due to natural processes, whirlwinds, bacteria or other physical processes he strongly asserted the statistical rarity of that is beyond measure. When asked about hoaxers, Douglas Bower and David Chorley, and whether they could have made these patterns he replied, "They could have, if they knew about the diatonic scale, and wished to put it in the circles. But I think we have to quote their reason for making the circles. They said they 'did it for a laugh.' That's fine. If they did it for a laugh, then it doesn't fit with putting in such an esoteric piece of information. I did write to them. They never replied."

ML: "You wrote to them saying what?"

GH: "Why did you put diatonic ratios in?"

ML: "And they didn't reply?"

GH: "No. I think we can eliminate them. It's so difficult to make a diatonic ratio. It has to be laid out accurately to within a few inches with a 50-foot circle, for example."

ML: "And many if not all of these circles were created at night."

GH: "Yes. Mostly they seem to be created at night."

Later Hawkins is asked about his major discovery, Euclid's 13th theorem, and whether he has an intellectual profile of the hoaxers.

"The suspected hoaxers are very erudite and knowledgeable in mathematics . . . There's more to this than just the diatonic ratio . . . Undiscovered theorems."

ML: "How so?"

GH: "Very interesting examples of pure geometry, or Euclidean geometry."

ML: "You found Euclidean theorems demonstrated in these other patterns?"

GH: "These are plane geometry, Euclidean theorems, *but they are not in Euclid's 13 books* [emphasis mine]. Everybody agrees that they are, by definition, theorems. But there's a big debate now between people who say that Euclid missed them, and those that say he didn't care about them — in other words, that the theorems are not important. I believe that Euclid missed them. They should be in Book 13, after proposition 12. There he had a very complicated theorem. These would just naturally follow. Another reason why he missed them was that we are pretty sure that he didn't know the full set of perfect diatonic ratios in 300 BC." Asked if these unknown Euclidian theorems were now widely accepted, Hawkins replied that they were, but only after he published them. Up to that time, "they were unknown."

Asked if he had any other discoveries about the more recent formations, his reply was somewhat modest: "Now we enter the other types of patterns — the pictograms, the insectograms. Exit Gerald S. Hawkins. I don't know what to do about those . . . I haven't gotten anywhere. I see no recognizable mathematical features."

The interviewer then asked if other scientists were working in this area, Hawkins surprised the interviewer by saying "No. It boils down to two factors. You wouldn't get a grant to study this sort of thing. And, two, *it might endanger your tenure. It is as serious as that*" [emphasis mine].[16]

Post-Hawkins

Since this 1992 interview, a few reputable journals have published a smattering of experimental studies.[17] One research group near Harvard calling itself "BLT research" reports controlled studies of grains inside and outside the crop circle with ostensibly reliable data showing the crop circles were not made in a mechanical way with boards or PVC pipe. Here is an excerpt:

> The data, however, rule out direct mechanical flattening of the crop circle plants by human beings utilizing planks or boards as an explanation for this event. Control studies carried out by BLT over the last several years have shown that significant node-length increase and expulsion cavities do not occur in crop flattened by boards or planks, human feet, or cement rollers, or to crop which has been 100% over-fertilized. And, since either geologic pressure and/or intense heat is required to cause decrease in KI of the clay minerals—and neither can be produced by planks, boards, cement rollers, feet, etc.—this, or a similar mechanical mechanism, must be ruled out. It is our intent to carry out additional plant and soil

research in an attempt to replicate the results that appear to have been designed with some kind of heat or radiation methodology. [18]

Such work is to be applauded, but we must admit that there has been little scientific interest overall. That is not to say that a totally intriguing subject matter is not waiting in the wings for future inquiries.

Crop Circle with *Pi*

The mysterious and intricate crop circle to the right appeared in a barley field near Wroughton in England in 2008. While it stood as simply one of many complex, fascinating designs, a retired astrophysicist, Mike Reed, tried mightily to decipher it. He succeeded and published his work in the prestigious, journal *Science*. In a delightful moment of insight he discovered it encoded *pi* to ten digits or actually 3.141592654 . . . to infinity.

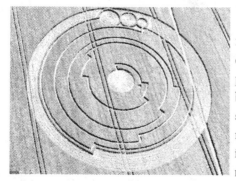

"The little dot near the center is the decimal point," he explains. "The code is based on 10 angular segments, with the radial jumps being the indicator of each segment." The three largest circles on the edge represent an ellipsis indicating that pi's absolute value extends toward an unknown infinity. [19]

Chilbolton

Even more awe-inspiring is a mysterious crop circle that appeared in Chilbolton, England (photo). Unlike in design to any of its predecessors, this formation appeared near a large radio telescope and seemed to be made out of pixels. [20]

It did not take researchers long to recognize that it bore an uncanny resemblance to a message sent out by radio telescope from the Arecibo radio observatory in 1974. This was a message coded and developed by the late Carl Sagan as an attempt to communicate with other species.

Since this is an utterly complex discussion, let us begin first by looking at the message from Arecibo which *we* sent out in 1974:

The Arecibo radio telescope dish . . . is the largest in the world. The most interesting experiment in 1974 with Arecibo however was its 3 Terawatt narrowband transmission of a "human template" in the direction of the M13 globular star cluster which consists of 300,000 stars and is in the constellation of Hercules."

The Arecibo template and how to read it are described next: The human template transmission (image) was made originally by Frank Drake with cooperation from astronomer Carl Sagan, whose book later was made into the movie "Contact." The journey of the template message from Arecibo would take 22,800 light years to reach Messier 13. The human template in 1974 was sent at the speed of light and in binary form. The Arecibo message included, among other things, the binary equivalent of the numbers 1–10, showing that a "base of 10" identified our math system and showing a way to decipher the message. Below these numbers, we identified the most common atomic numbers in life that we knew at that time. We transmitted our atomic numbers for Hydrogen, Carbon, Nitrogen, Oxygen and Phosphorus. We didn't stop there and added the molecular formulas for our human DNA (Deoxyribonucleic Acid). We also sent, as the human race, our average height, and a rough proportional representation of our bodies. The population of our planet earth in 1974 was estimated at 4.29 billion humans and this was also transmitted. For the source of the transmission, planet Earth, Arecibo, we sent our solar system identifying the third planet from the Sun —Earth — just under our feet. Also with the source was the Arecibo Telescope and its diameter. Expecting the transmission to take 22,800 light years might have been an exaggeration when, in reality, it could reach some other life forms much earlier. In fact, the transmission has now traveled nearly 27 light years from Earth (156 trillion + miles) — towards M13 and has passed the distance of the closest star from our Sun which is 4.3 light years away.[21]

Below we compare the Chilbolton crop circle (left) and the Arecibo message on the right. Paul Vigay renders a stunning interpretation:

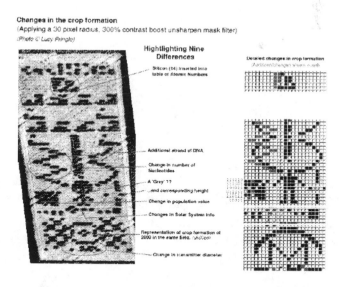

Changes in the crop formation
(Applying a 30 pixel radius, 300% contrast boost unsharpen mask filter)
(Photo © Lucy Pringle)

Highlighting Nine Differences

Silicon (14) inserted into table of Atomic Numbers

Additional strand of DNA

Change in number of Nucleotides

A 'Grey' ??

...and corresponding height

Change in population value

Changes in Solar System Info

Representation of crop formation of 2000 in the same field.

Change in transmitter diameter

Detailed changes in crop formation

"The numbers 1 to 10 appear exactly the same in the formation. However the atomic numbers indicating the prevalent elements making up life on Earth has an additional value inserted into the binary sequence. This is precisely added in the correct location, and in the original binary code . . . Decoding from the crop formation, this additional element has an atomic number of 14 = Silicon.

Moving down, the next change is an obvious one — consisting of an extra strand on the left side of the obvious, change is in the binary coding of the number of nucleotides in DNA itself (in the center) . . . There are quite significant changes to the shape of the humanoid, which becomes almost 'alien-like' and to the diagram of the Arecibo dish . . . There are changes to both the 'population' figure and also the height value. The latter is . . . roughly 3'4" (three feet four inches) . . . Below this we notice additional changes to the Solar System chart. The third planet from the sun is not the only one 'highlighted' now. The fourth and fifth are as well. The fifth even appears to be emphasized even more, with three additional 'pixels' . . . If you decode the 'population' binary sequence in the actual crop formation you get a value of approximately 21.3 billion — a lot bigger than the original transmission . . . There is also some indication of a change in the basic DNA structure . . . . The additional (third) strand shown on the left and also a change in the number of nucleotides indicates a different DNA to ours." [Source: Paul Vigay, 26th August, 2000 http://www.cropcircleresearch.com/articles/arecibo.html]

Is it possible the first message sent to us from alien beings has been decoded? The Arecibo transmission did not simply go out into space in 1974. It was rebroadcast in the 1990s from our spacecraft.

If the Chilbolton formation is really a hoax, it was certainly crafted with diligence, enormous creativity, a macabre sense of humor, and beguiling ingenuity by creating a pixel-like crop formation without leaving the hint of a footprint. But if it is genuine, preliminary interpretations would suggest that our alien cousins live in a solar system of nine planets, comprise a society with a population of 21 billion beings, possess similar DNA which involves silicon in some manner, and are approximately 3.5 feet tall![22]

Conclusion

Frankly, drawing conclusions that crop circles are the work of the Gods or extraterrestrials carving out messages using balls of light is unwarranted at this stage of our knowledge. At the same time, assuming all crop circles are hoaxes made with PVC pipe by people "doing it for a laugh" seems equally unjustified.

Surely many will continue to interpret the burgeoning growth of crop circles as a devilish human activity or a creative new form of landscape art. Others think our multiple transmissions into outer space and attempts to communicate are finally reaping rewards as ever more complex crop circles appear in the most awesome designs . . . most yet to surrender themselves to any decoding.

There have been interpretations of crop circles as fractals, Mandelbrot sets, or variations on the Flower of Life, but the complexity of these figures is far greater than the meager interpretive renditions obtained so far. Unfortunately — and with considerable regret— there is a profusion of New Age, spiritualist blathering about mystical-escoteric-ethereal-orgone-energy-plasma-physics-vortices that just makes your head spin.[23] At the same time there is an absolute dearth of genuine, peer-reviewed scientific interest. This text agrees with Professor Hawkins that scientific inquiry is not only justified and legitimate but necessary. As he said before his death:

> There are whole areas in the scientific community that are not informed about the crop circle phenomenon, and have come to the conclusion that it is ridiculous, a hoax, a joke, and a waste of time. It's a difficult topic because it tends to raise a knee-jerk solution in people's minds. Then they are stuck. Their minds are closed. One can't do much about it. But if they can keep an open mind, I think they'll find they've got a very interesting phenomenon.[24]

Hopefully one day we will see analytic inquiries into these designs by astronomers, physicists, and molecular biologists, similar to the work of astrophysicist Mike Reed and Professor Dawkins, and perhaps tease out other undiscovered theorems or formulae from this breathtaking complexity.

This, then, completes another leg of our exploration of the extraterrestrial hypothesis. We hve looked into the archeological, mythological, and paranormal rooms in our ET museum. Finally, we venture down the hall to consider whether there is any merit to the supposition that *Homo sapiens* may have had its genome tinkered with by outside agitators.

If Doug and Dave hoaxed the circles, they deserve a Nobel Prize!
—Richard Hoagland, author of *The Monuments of Man*

Endnotes

1 Andrew Collins. *The New Circlemakers*, Virginia Beach: 4th Dimension Press, 2009.

2 Eltjo Haselhoff, *Crop Circles: Scientific Research & Urban Legends*, Berkeley, CA: North Atlantic Books, 2001

3 The incident occurred in Fairfield, California on July 3, 2003. See Leslie Kean "California crop circles add to scientific mystery." Global Village News: http://www.gvnr.com/66/1.htm

4 Andrew Collins. *Ibid.*.

5 Eltjo Haselhoff, *Ibid.*, pp. 7-8.

6 Freddy Silva, *Secrets in the fields*, Charlottesville, VA: Hampton Roads Publishing, 2002, p. xii.

7 *Nature*; 7/04/96, Vol. 382 Issue 6586, p3

8 http://freakyphenomena.com/news/2008/12/15/most-puzzling-crop-circles

9 Haselhoff, *Ibid.*, p. 16.

10 A more detailed investigation of the fly mystery is given at Crop Circles, the dead flies mystery, June, 2003; http://www.cicap.org/crops/en/006.htm

11 Cited from an internet source: www.zetatalk.com/theword/twordo2e.htm.

12 Haselhoff, *Ibid.*, p. 89.

13 A particularly impressive set of examples of this phenomena are found in Figures 8.8 and 8.9 of Silva's text, *Secrets in the Fields, Ibid.*, 2002, p. A9.

14 Haselhoff, *Ibid.*, p. 58.

15 Haselhoff, *Ibid.*, p. 63.

16 This interview first appeared in Share International's December, 1992 edition.

17 A list of world-wide research groups is given at the following URL: http://www.bltresearch.com/general.php#videos.

18 http://www.bltresearch.com/xrd.php#disc. See also *Journal of Scientific Exploration*, Vol. 9, No. 2, pp. 191-199, 1995.

19 The Most "Mind Boggling" Crop Circle. British Heritage, 01952633, Nov2008, Vol. 29, Issue 5 See also Science; 6/27/2008, Vol. 320 Issue 5884, p1701-1701, 1/4p. A second, color-coded explanation of this circle can be found at http://allnews.com/222/crop-circle-depicts-pi/.

20 Many crop circles seem to appear near either radio telescopes or ancient mounds and monoliths like Stonehenge.

21 Source: http://amo.net/Contact/By Dustin D. Brand

22 Over ten independent UFO reports say aliens were seen who were under four feet tall. [See Alien Encounters, *Ibid.*, and Timothy Good's Need to Know. *Ibid.*

23 See Andrew Collins, *The New Circlemakers*, Ibid., 2009

24 http://www.share-international.org/archives/crop_circles/cc_ml-music-spheres. htm. Courtesy of Share International Magazine. Articles may be reproduced, free of charge, with credit to Share International magazine, P.O. Box 971, N. Hollywood, CA 91603 USA, www.share-international.org.

6. Biological Evidence for Extraterrestrial Contact

> *The Nephilim were on the earth in those*
> *days—and also afterward—when the*
> *sons of God went to the daughters of*
> *men and had children by them.*
> *Genesis 6:1-5*

There is a pervasive theme in human mythology and in its myriad creation myths that goes beyond mere visitations by other beings but speaks of Gods who mate with man or who biologically altered our species. This theme is found in myths in China, Greece, Rome, Sumeria, Germany, and *Genesis*.

Before exploring this last frontier of evidence, take a step back with me and think through this quotation from psychoanalyst Karl Abraham:

> And just as certain psychic products of the healthy and sick in-
> dividual are reminiscent of that early stage of his childhood, so in
> its legends and fairy tales does the race as a whole preserve the
> traces of its remotest past.[1]

Abraham's idea is one, which we have been concerned with in this book, namely that ancient tales and myths *encode* human experiences and preserve them from ancient times.

"Ring around the rosy, pocket full of posy," traces back to the bubonic plague, which ravaged Europe in the fourteenth century.[2] Children sing these verses and, in turn, pass on a collective memory trace to the next generation, generally entirely unconscious of the roots and origins of this human trauma.

When we ask why this process occurs, our best answer seems to be that oral cultural transmission though myth, fable, fairy tale, and metaphor has some adaptive significance, as if the recitation and transmission of the rhyme recalls an event, a disease, or a condition which was threatening to mankind. When twenty five percent of the European population died from the Black Death, a symbolic ring-around-the-rosy memory trace seems propitious from the standpoint of evolutionary psychology.

But these rhymes may be more than that. During the devastating "Spanish flu"[3] of 1918, a worldwide pandemic which took at least thirty million lives, a nursery rhyme appeared:

> I had a little bird
> And its name was Enza
> I opened the window
> And influEnza.

President Wilson, who almost succumbed to the disease, murmured this verse in the Oval office, as did so many others across the nation. More than half a million Americans died in the epidemic in a ravaging nine months, far exceeding American casualties in World War I. The rhyme not only memorializes the event, but its most elegant component is that it actually hints that the disease was "bird borne."

In 1918 viruses had not yet been isolated and they weren't known until 1931. There was no conscious suspicion that disease could be spread by birds. Current research on this plague took extracts of frozen tissue from the preserved cadavers of victims of the 1918 flu and showed it to be a variant of swine flu.[4]

What we now know is that Canada geese migrating south excreted droppings on Midwestern farms, which were absorbed by pigs. The bird-borne virus then incubated, mutated, and was passed on to human beings, eventually infecting the entire world. The rhyme about the bird, *Enza,* not only recalls the event, but provides a diagnostic clue, completely unrecognized in 1918, that the pandemic was of avian origin, *as it indeed was.*

Kirlian Photography and *Ch'i*

By placing a living object directly on a photographic plate and running an electric current through it, what appears looks remarkably like an aura. First discovered in 1937 and known as Kirlian photography, the aura was most easily observable from a fingerprint. The fingerprint-aura is generally colored blue, and alters its size depending on various mood states.[5] If a psychiatric patient is in a manic state, it was expansive and pinkish; if depressed, it contracts into a deeper bluish tint. The size, coloring, and character also varies with a woman's ovulatory cycle.[6]

Kirlian Fingerprint Photo

It is uncanny that prior to the discovery to Kirlian auras, *ninety-six* different cultures mentioned auras, halos, and egg-shaped bubbles of iridescence surrounding the human body. These descriptions can be found in the medieval writings of Christian mystics, the sacred works of ancient India describing *prana,* as well as China in the third millennium BC where the concept of *ch'i* is first mentioned. Even though science had not verifiably recorded *any such evidence until 1937,* the prescience of mythology antedated modern science by some five thousand years.[7]

Sort of creates a new respect for the ancient record.

Most scientists relegated the concept of auras and halos to the dustbin of superstitious folklore and never gave it a second thought. That same attitude holds true for much of what we will be discussing next, the possibility that the *Homo sapiens* genome has been tweaked in some manner through extraterrestrial interaction. Are these accountings mere superstitious, delusory attempts to give our species a divine veneer and a cosmic importance, or are these mythic reports of interaction between man and the Gods archaic memories?

Man as Hybrid

The lyrics of an ancient Greek (Orphic) song are, "I am a child of Earth and starry Heaven, but my race is of Heaven.[8] In Sumeria the earth goddess Ki mates with the heavenly god, An, and from their intercourse comes Enlil.[9] Enlil, in turn, 1,500 years before the Old Testament, reports in the saga of *Gilgamesh* of the great flood and an ark that was built according to specifications given by the gods.

In India the gods Shiva and Devi were involved in the creation of human beings. The royal family of Japan is said to have descended from an incestuous conception of the gods. In Ireland the goddess Danann gave birth to Bres, who was "given the kingship of Ireland."[10] In the Book of Noah and the Book of Enoch there are "explicit accounts of physical intercourse between the gods and humans."[11] In Christian mythology, the Spirit of God impregnates Mary and begets Jesus, half man, half god.

> Greek legends delight in the amorous revels of Zeus descending as a hero, bull, even a swan, to seduce any willing maid: Mars ravished the Vestal Virgin, Rhea Silvia to father Romulus; the Gods and Goddesses of Old India winged down for pleasure with mortals procreating Kings; the Babylonian Beauty Queen won a date with Marduk in that elegant boudoir topping his great Temple; the Japanese Emperors claimed descent from Amaterasu, Goddess of the Sun . . . Jehovah's visitation to the beauteous Sarah produced Isaac, father of Jacob . . . Such unions between Celestials and Earthmen and Earthwomen may not have been the lust we imagine but divine eugenics to create a new race.[12]

Just as 'ring around the rosy' points to the bubonic plague and the numerous flood myths may encode a memory of deglaciation from the last ice age, is it possible that such creation-interbreeding myths have a similar meaning and significance and represent archaic memories of actual events?

Evolutionary Biology

We were taught that the process of evolution is gradual, that man came down a special evolutionary tree, and that the ultimate manifestation of *Homo sapiens* is a logical, and slow process of evolution and natural selection. In elementary school we eagle-eyed drawings of apes walking behind a two-legged, upright hirsute Neanderthal, followed by other developing hominids until finally *Homo sapiens* appears as the end point of an evolution occurring over millions of years. And sometimes he was even wearing a tie.

In the last fifteen years numerous findings impugn our traditional notions. One problem is whether we are actually descended from Neanderthal. A second is that we seem to be far older than we ever thought. A third involves the recent appearance of a DNA anomaly called Mungo Man, and the final issue sucks us into the conundrum of how the evolution of human *culture* does not seem to advance in a way paralleling our physical evolution. We will take up all these four topics in this chapter.

Neanderthal Kith and Kin?

Current evidence suggests that Neanderthal is only a distant cousin. A Neanderthal bone discovered some time ago was examined for retrievable DNA. Some was found, and it shows Neanderthal was not the forefather of *H. sapiens* and genetically distinct.[13]

The finding, by veteran ancient-DNA researcher Svante Paabo of Munich and his colleagues, could help bring down the curtain on one of the longest running and feud-prone disputes in anthropology: whether Neanderthals disappeared . . . because they gradually evolved into modern humans; or whether they were abruptly superseded by an evolutionary strain that left Af-

rica only a few dozen millenniums ago and from which all people now alive are descended.[14]

It seems that *Homo erectus* was the common ancestor and that Neanderthals and modern humans evolved separately.

Another study reports Neanderthal DNA differs from human and chimpanzee DNA in 27 different ways[15] and that *Homo sapiens* and Neanderthal never mated.[16]

Recent findings from Indonesia in 1996 show that *Homo erectus*, was around as late as 53,000 years ago. This means that *Homo erectus* and *Homo sapiens* co-existed. One researcher says all three co-existed:

> It now seems that three separate human species—Neanderthals, anatomically modern humans, and an older species called *Homo erectus*—apparently coexisted until as recently as 30,000 years ago in part of Europe and Asia.[17]

But there is some contrary evidence too. A "hybrid" four-year old boy was found in 1999 that was approximately 24,500 years old. He was part Neanderthal and part early modern *Homo sapiens.* The find pushes Neanderthal existence ahead 4,000 years, but stirs up the controversy over whether Neanderthal might have interbred with *Homo sapiens.*[18]

A follow-up investigation contradicts that. Using DNA extracted from the "perfectly preserved bones of a Neanderthal infant girl who died about 30,000 years ago" and comparing that to another Neanderthal sample discovered in 1997, "the two Neanderthal samples turned out to be just 3.5 percent different from one another, they were roughly 7 percent different from DNA in modern humans."[19]

Conclusion once again: Neanderthals and humans were distinctly different and one did not evolve out of the other.[20]

[By the way, Neanderthal actually was taller and had a larger brain than H. sapiens by about 100 cc].[21]

The most recent research comes from a 2009 study from the Max Planck Institute for Evolutionary Anthropology. They decoded 3.7 billion bases of Neanderthal DNA from a female bone found in Croatia. One interesting finding was that Neanderthals shared a version of the FOXP2 gene related to speech, and this is the best indication so far that Neanderthals could speak. Comparison with both human and chimp DNA, however, showed Neanderthal had a closer relationship to chimps than humans do and that they "contributed very little if anything" to the genetic make-up of modern humans, arguing again that interbreeding was either non-existent or minimal.[22]

How Old Are We?

A second shock to our traditional understanding of evolution concerns just how old we are. First *Homo sapiens* differs from *Homo sapiens sapiens*, the former referred to as 'archaic' and latter as 'anatomically modern.'[23] Cro-Magnon is a term used for the early or archaic *Homo sapiens*

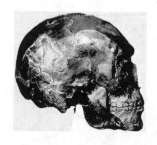

Omo I skull considered a modern H. sapiens and dated at 196,000 years

For the date for which fully modern Homo sapiens appears we go to the laboratories of the famed Steven Jay Gould. From this group in an article entitled "Out of Africa vs. Multiregionalism," Tod Billings reviews the literature searching for the oldest known *Homo sapiens sapiens*.[24] Some skulls date between 92,000 and 115,000 years, while the Skhul fossils in Israel date from 80,000–119,000 years, and yet another from the same collection dates to 130,000 years.[25][26]

Earlier textbooks placed anatomically modern man at only about 50,000 years of age, but the best evidence now pushes that date back to 130,000 years and counting. In fact the Omo skull, discovered in 1967, was redated in 2005 at 196,000 years of age, also an anatomically modern *Homo sapiens!*[27]

A study published in *Nature* in February, 2005 using isotopic analysis of volcanic ash above and below the finds reports "our species, *Homo sapiens*, has a new pair of ultimate old-timers" and reports the age of both Omo I and II skulls at 196,000 years.[28]

For the remainder of this chapter, however, we will generally use the more conservative 130,000 year dateline for purposes of consistency, but 196,000 years is a very good, contemporary guesstimate of our actual age.[29]

Mungo Man, Chimps, and *H. sapiens*

The third problem concerns recently discovered Mungo Man. Let us get some background first on our DNA and chimps before we begin this discussion.

Differences in DNA between *Homo sapiens and* chimpanzees are approximately 0.6–1.4 percent. Some authors have speculated that of the 30,000 genes in biologically modern *Homo sapiens*, only about 300 or 1 percent differ significantly from chimpanzees.[30] [31] [32]

A recent study looked at 97 specific genes to see what differences appeared between humans and chimps. This investigation revealed we have an even closer association with chimps sharing 99.4 percent of their DNA.[33] A more recent study using a different counting method, however, suggested that overall there might be as much as a *five percent* difference and thus only a 95 percent similarity between human and chimp DNA.[34]

The traditional argument, to which most of us were exposed, was that in the 4.8 million years separating chimps and us, a gradual evolutionary creep pushed inexorably forward where incipient biologically modern man differentiated out greater cranial capacity and a more advanced neurology. All of that culminated in the emergence of cognitively superior, anatomically superior *Homo sapiens*.

Thus, the meager one- to five-percent genetic difference between chimps and man is the genomic *platform* upon which evolutionary biology explains how *Homo sapiens* emerged to take over and change the entire character of the planet.

Recently a discovery reported a 60,000-year-old *H. sapiens* skeleton, called Mungo Man. It is the oldest human skeleton ever to provide viable DNA. Morphologically a biologically modern man, its DNA was *substantially different from* our own, "something scientists had not expected and like nothing they have ever seen before."[35]

> Mungo Man became the oldest human fossil that was physically similar to modern humans. But further analysis of Mungo's mitochondrial DNA (mtDNA) could not link him to any human population living today.[36]

> The ANU's John Curtin School of Medical Research found that Mungo Man's skeleton's contained a small section of mitochondrial DNA. After analyzing the DNA, the school found that Mungo Man's DNA bore no similarity to the other ancient skeletons, modern Aborigines and modern Europeans.[37]

Some argue that Mungo Man could not have migrated out of Africa and thus different lineages of *Homo sapiens* independently emerged (the multiregional hypothesis).

Other researchers believe that differing variants of *Homo sapiens* existed, some becoming extinct like Mungo Man. Ian Tattersall and Jeffrey Schwartz say fifteen different species of humans may have existed over time where Mungo Man would merely be one example.[38] Others strongly and stridently object to the idea of multiple and different sub-species[39] and say only a single group migrated out of Africa some 100,000 years ago.[40]

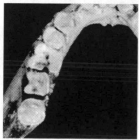

Mungo Man skeleton and jaw

Mungo Man is controversial. The evidence and DNA dating have been reviewed and the re-reviewed. The current opinion on this subject still holds that his DNA is far different from current *Homo sapiens* DNA, but the age of the specimen now has been re-dated at 42,000 years.[41]

Let us summarize our discussion up to this point: (1) *Homo sapiens* does not appear related to Neanderthal, did not evolve from him, but was his contemporary up to about 30,000 years ago.[42] (2) *Homo sapiens* evolved from *Homo erectus*, our most immediate ancestor, and biologically modern man has been here for between 130–196,000 years. (3) The oldest anatomically modern *Homo sapiens* DNA ever retrieved, 42,000 year-old Mungo Man, differs substantially in its DNA profile from modern humans.

The Evolution of Human Culture.

Although there is some meager evidence to show Neanderthal may have used stone tools, the origin of complex human symbolic behavior is recent and drastic. If we date *Homo sapiens* cognitive superiority to empirically observable tangible behavior i.e., technology, written language, buildings, cities, and the first emergence of what we call culture and civilization, then our precocity is roughly 6,000–10,000 years old. That represents a *fraction* of the evolutionary time separating chimpanzees and man (about 2 one hundredths of one percent), and, in fact, only a fraction of the time *Homo sapiens* has walked this planet.

Here is a more practical glimpse of the issue. In this instance it concerns a stunning observation about Egyptian hieroglyphs:

> . . . Remains from the pre-dynastic period around 3500 BC show no trace of writing. Soon after that date, quite suddenly and inexplicably, the hieroglyphs familiar from so many of the ruins of Ancient Egypt begin to appear in a complete and perfect state. Far from being mere pictures of objects or actions, this written language was complex and structured at the outset, with signs that represented sounds only and a detailed system of numerical symbols. . . and it is clear that an advanced cursive script was in common usage by the dawn of the First Dynasty . . . What is remarkable is that there are no traces of evolution from simple to sophisticated, and the same is true of mathematics, medicine,

astronomy, and architecture . . . even the central content of such refined works as the *Book of the Dead* existed right at the start of the dynastic period . . .

According to John Anthony West, an expert on the early dynastic period,

> How does a complex civilization spring full blown into being? Look at a 1905 automobile and compare it to a modern one. This is no mistaking the process of development. But in Egypt there are no parallels. Everything is right there from the start.[43]

Where are the precursors to the hieroglyphs? And where are the documents spanning at least a couple millennia corroborating a *gradual and progressive* development of hieroglyphs, pyramid building, mathematics, and astronomy?

If we are to explain all this using the traditional route, namely that some kind of genetic mutations happened which gave rise to our cognitive superiority, then we have to confront some gnarly issues. How did we get so smart *so quickly* if we have been around as long as we have?

If we share between 95–99 percent our DNA with chimps, and the one to five percent differentiation[44] took 5 million years of evolution to accomplish, our differences in brain size, tool use, language development, and cognitive capacity should all be explained by these same genetic differences. If so, then we have to imagine rather dramatic mutations (a) *in an extremely small portion of our DNA* and (b) *in the very, very recent past,* only the last 4–7 percent of our total time walking these continents.

While you are doing the genomic gymnastics to think through that puzzle, consider what Carl Sagan says about the evolution of our big toe:

> The time scale for evolutionary or genetic change is very long. A characteristic period for the emergence of one advanced species from another is perhaps a hundred thousand years; and very often the differences in behavior between closely related species— say, lions and tigers—do not seem very great. An example of recent evolution of organ systems in humans is our toes. The big toe

plays an important function in balance while walking; the other toes have much less obvious utility. They are clearly evolved from fingerlike appendages for grasping and swinging, like those of arboreal apes and monkeys. This evolution constitutes a respecialization—the adaptation of an organ system originally evolved for one function to another and quite different function—which required about ten million years to emerge. The feet of the mountain gorilla have undergone a similar although quite independent evolution.[45]

If it takes over a hundred thousand years to differentiate out a human big toe from a chimpanzee big toe, how can we use evolutionary biology to explain the *virtually instantaneous* emergence of human culture? Again from Carl Sagan:

> ...the Neanderthals and the Cro-Magnons[46] . . . had average brain volumes of about 1,500 cubic centimeters; that is, more than a hundred cubic centimeters larger than ours. Most anthropologists guess that we are not descended from Neanderthals and may not be from Cro-Magnons either. But their existence raises the question: Who were those fellows? What were their accomplishments? Cro-Magnon was also very large: some specimens were well over six feet tall . . . Chimpanzees have large brains: they have well-developed neocortices; they, too, have long childhoods and extended periods of plasticity. Are they capable of abstract thought?

Of all the hominids which diverged from chimpanzees, only one shows evidence of consummate intellectual gifts. The whole planet shivers and shakes as *H. sapiens* marches across its surface. From our first recorded civilization until the present, planet earth was altered, electrified, mined, industrialized, overpopulated, deforested, polluted, and warmed to the point of melting ice sheets at both poles *in less than ten millennia*, but our anatomically modern species has been here—at the latest count—for 196 millennia!

The hurdle over which evolutionary biology must jump is to explain this breakneck pace by a mysterious set of genetic mutations all occurring within that narrow band of DNA difference between ourselves and chimpanzees and in the narrowest chunk of Darwinian time possible.

Something does not fit! [See Fig 6.1 for a summary of this discussion].

Fig. 6.1 Chimpanzee and Homo sapiens evolution

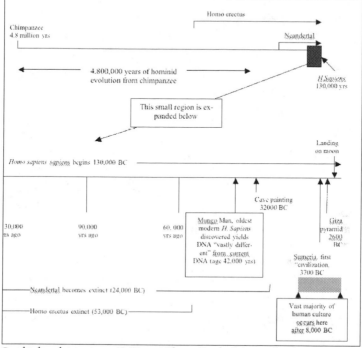

Graphic based, in part, on K. Wong, "African Exodus," Scientific American, Nov 2000, pp. 82-83.

Traditional Explanations

The Development of Agriculture

Let us first review what traditional anthropology says about this conundrum. In *Non Zero, The Logic Of Human Destiny*,[47] Robert Wright explains mankind's dearth of culture for such a long period of his history. The essence of his argument is that as evolution manipulates genes to move toward greater complexity (single-celled to multicellular), cultural evolution uses 'memes' or ideas/innovations, which spread from the simple to complex in very similar fashion.

The spread is like a virus and disseminates through the human population steadily finally reaching exponential proportion. Thus human populations start small bereft of any major technological innovations, and then one meme starts to appear about every 20,000 years, followed by others every 1400 years, until finally newer advancements happen every 200 years (like the invention of the comb). In this way Wright uses what he calls "ascending non-zero sum complexity" to explain the *hastening* of human culture, and by that he means through the exponential acceleration of cultural memes and innovations.

Moving from tribe to village, village to city, city to chiefdom, and chiefdom to empire represents another ascending series of memes which grow from simple to more complex. Wright places great emphasis on the development of agriculture spurring human innovation, beginning between 7,000 BC to 10,000 BC. This allowed more people to be freed from food gathering, created a larger, more sedentary and dense human population, and paved the way for even more innovations like writing, pottery, smelting, and science.[48]

One reason Wright's argument seems unconvincing is that it did not really take 200 years to develop a comb. It took over 100,000 years from biologically modern *Homo sapiens* first appearance until the day he recognized he was having a bad hair day and decided to treat the condition.

Wright ignores the biological issue that if *Homo sapiens* was biologically intact 130,000 years ago—in terms of cortical development, for example—why did cultural memes of any genuine significance not really start appearing until the third and fourth millennium BC? Wright's book *explains away* the very abrupt beginnings of human culture by stretching them out and extrapolating backwards in order to give cultural evolution a patina it doesn't deserve. In this way the impetuous beginnings of human culture are made to seem gradual, progressive, and the result of an ersatz uniformitarianism.[49]

The Frontal Lobes

Let's try another traditional approach:

This time a biological argument is used. *Homo sapiens,* it is said, has a significantly larger frontal cortex, and this represents the *sine qua non* for the human cultural big bang. The expanse of the frontal lobes, compared to other primates, has been the mother lode from which most contemporary explanations flow. Supercharged, *Homo Sapiens* frontal lobes historically provided the base for a geometric progression in conceptual, symbolic thinking, and *this single feature* differentiates us from lower primates including Neanderthal.

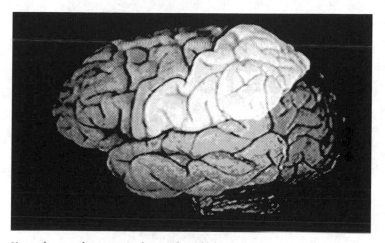

Human brain with gray area indicating frontal lobes

Unfortunately this explanation has to confront some rather recent bitter facts. Researchers at the California Institute of Technology report:

> . . . researchers have traditionally theorized that the frontal cortex, a brain region linked to mental faculties such as planning and reasoning, expanded to an unprecedented extent during human evolution. However, a new analysis of brains from many different mammals takes the uniqueness out of our frontal cortex. Lemurs, gibbons, chimpanzees, and other primates have roughly the same proportion of brain tissue devoted to the frontal cortex as people do, say Eliot C. Bush and John M. Allman of the California Institute of Technology in Pasadena. Lions, hyenas, and other carnivores display a substantially smaller frontal cortex relative to the rest of the brain.

... Bush and Allman widened the scope of frontal cortex analysis, focusing on primates and carnivores. They compared 25 primate species with 15 carnivore species. Computerized analyses of a series of brain slices identified various neural regions and yielded volume estimates for them.

In all the primates, the frontal cortex displayed about the same relative size, approximately 36 percent of the total brain volume, while carnivores had less than 30 percent of their brain in this area.

Intriguingly, lemurs and other prosimians—regarded as the most primitive primate suborder—exhibited a slightly greater frontal cortex proportion than people and great apes did. That finding challenges the influential theory that the frontal cortex progressively expanded in our primate ancestors, Bush holds.[50]

Traditional arguments have problems, and many anthropologists admit to ardent head-scratching in trying to answer why human culture happened as quickly as it did after such a long period of dormancy.

But mythology sits quietly off in the corner with its own rendition of these affairs. Let's take a closer look:

The Mythological Theory Expressed

Let us recast the essence of the 'alien-hybrid' hypothesis we have been thinking about in this chapter. It took 5 million years to quadruple the size of a chimpanzee brain so that it would fit neatly into a *Homo sapiens* skull. We have a remarkable propinquity to our simian cousins,[51] but a distinct behavioral difference separates us from them. Consider what chimps do now, today, after 5 million years of evolution:

Among things they've been seen doing: throwing rocks at leopards; attacking a fake leopard with sticks, taking twigs, stripping them of leaves, poking them down into a termite nest, then pulling them out and eating the termites; pounding nuts open with sticks and stones. Chimps even use sticks to brush each other's teeth. Some chimps crumple up leaves, turning them into sponges with which to extract precious water from the hollows of trees. Chimps also use leaves to wipe the last bits of delicious brain from the skulls of freshly killed baboons.[52]

Bon appetit! But is this the entire panorama of their intellectual and cognitive repertoire? Not quite. Other studies report chimpanzees engage in twenty-six different practices, behaviors, and rituals which are passed down from one sub-group to the next, and these behaviors qualify as fitting the definition of "culture," i.e., a learned trait that is passed exosomatically (non-biologically). So with chimpanzee culture and the twenty-six behaviors that took five million years to develop and evolve, how do we reconcile *Homo sapiens* cultural evolution with this?[53]

Just as the skull of 130,000-year-old *Homo sapiens sapiens* is like our skull now, it is probable his neocortex was like ours, too.

It is certainly logical to assume that when he first appeared right next to Neanderthal and *Homo erectus*, modern *Homo sapiens* had virtually the same brain size and cortical capacities that he has today. If true, then why was he so incredibly stupid?

Table 6.3 Late Bloomer

Invention/Advancement	Date first appeared	Years since beginning of Homo Sapiens sapiens*
Domesticated, goats & sheep	8500BC	119,500
First cities (Mesopotamia)	7500BC	120,500
Domesticated wheat	7250 BC	120,750
Domesticated pigs	7000 BC	121,000
Domesticated horses	4000 BC	124,000
Copper & bronze	4000 BC	124,000
Brewing beer	3500 BC	124,500
First written language	3500 BC	124,500
Stonehenge	3000 BC	124,000
Invention of wheel	3000 BC	124,000

*Using the age of biologically modern man at 130,000 years. Source for the table is adapted, in part, from Jared Diamond's *Guns, Germs & Steel*, NY: Norton, 2005.[54]

Why did it take 124,000 years to invent a wheel,[55] 120,000 years to think of domesticating plants to begin farming, or 121,000 years before he got the idea of domesticating animals which could till the earth and grow his crops?

Why did it take 124,000 years to create a written language or fashion copper and bronze? Why did he twiddle his Paleolithic thumbs for so long?

From 130,000 BC to about 30,000 BC, one really couldn't tell the behavioral or cognitive difference between Neanderthal and *Homo sapiens*. Both species used spears, harpoons, fish hooks, traps, hunted game in groups, used flaked stone tools, and neither displayed any evidence of having constructed significant living structures. If one could find significant empirical evidence that one species was clearly superior or smarter than the other in this Paleolithic period, say from 50,000–30,000 BC, it would be a stretch.

Neanderthal using stone tools

From 20,000 BC, *Homo sapiens sapiens* shows an incipient sophistication in his use of tools and hunting techniques, but it is not until about 8–4,000 BC that we start to see a flowering of human culture and the beginnings of what we now call 'civilization.'[56]

If we were clearly a far superior species intellectually, we might find *Homo sapiens* villages while Neanderthal languished in caves, but the record in Paleolithic times is muddled. In fact, in 30,000 BC Neanderthal and *Homo sapiens*' remains were found in the same cave in Saint Cezaire, France. To say that one species was superior to the other *then* is questionable. Multiple numbers of anthropologists make that clear. [57] [58]

In other words, the evidence shows that *we were as uninventive as they were*, and by present standards, Paleolithic, biologically modern *Homo sapiens* and Neanderthals both appear to be dullards.

Modern *Homo sapiens* reached China by 68,000 BC, Australia by 60,000 BC[59] and by that time had spread around most of the Old World, but we didn't codify a single written language . . . even by 3,500 BC!

> We know that 20,000 years ago all people up to that time, ap-proximately 100,000 generations—were hunter-gatherers living in simple egalitarian tribal units. By comparison, only 500 gen-erations in total have depended on agriculture, and only 10 gen-erations have lived in industrial civilization.[60]

That is a remarkable sudden growth spurt. In a flash everything changed. Our imbecilic IQ seems to double overnight. Consider what one author writes about Sumeria:

> Before the Sumerians there were no bakers, harpists, carpen-ters, jewelers, artists, engineers, mathematicians, bureaucrats, or scribes. All these innovations appeared for the first time in their cities between 3700 BC and 3000 BC. In addition to irrigation, kilns, and writing, they also invented the wheel, the chariot, bronze, sailboats, mathematics . . . astrology, schools, and the idea of trades and professions. In short, *they invented nearly the entire foundation of all future civilizations*—all in one fell swoop.[61]

Prior to 4,000 BC *Homo sapiens* generally lived as nomadic hunt-ers and gatherers, but in the blink of an eye, the Sumerian civiliza-tion popped up beginning around 3700 BC, and in addition to all of the above, a second author rhapsodizes further: They developed—and these were all firsts—

> . . . high rise buildings, streets, market places, granaries, wharves . . . temples, metallurgy, medicine, surgery, textile making, gour-met foods, the use of bricks . . . carts, ships and navigation; in-ternational trade; weights and measures; kingship, laws, courts, juries, writing and record keeping; music, musical notes, musical instruments, dance and acrobatics; domestic animals and zoos; warfare, artisanship, prostitution.[62]

One could make a very defensible assertion that the cognitive and intellectual achievements of *Homo sapiens* between 4,000–2,500 BC were more significant than in all the prior 124 millennia *combined!*

Think about that. In such a short period of time our adrenalized species struts out its cognitive stuff out like it's a fourth-of-July parade. Some kind of uncanny metamorphosis converts him into an awesome paragon of innovation. He builds cities, creates the highly complex and elaborate language of Egyptian hieroglyphics, boasts a staggering knowledge of astronomy, encrypts *pi* and *Phi* in the Pyramid of Giza, and manages in 2,600 BC—some say earlier some earlier—to engineer a pyramid that uses two million blocks of stone, enough to enclose St. Peter's, St. Paul's, and the cathedrals of Florence, Milan, and Westminster combined![63]

> Over two million limestone blocks rise to the height of a forty-story building. Each baseline exceeds two and a half football fields. Standing on top, an archer cannot clear the base with an arrow . . . Occupying an area of thirteen acres, the entire bedrock base has been carved to less than an inch out of level. It is oriented within a tiny fraction of a degree from the cardinal points. Outer casing stones and inner granite blocks fit with such precision that a razor blade cannot be inserted between them. Blocks weighing as much as seventy tons (about what a railroad locomotive weighs) have been lifted to the height of a ten-story building and mated to the next block with wondrous precision . . . All this comes from what was supposedly an agrarian society, forty-five hundred years ago.[64]

The Great Pyramid

One of the very first structures built by man, it used stones hewn and moved by processes still under debate even in the 21st century. The building even appears to encode the perihelion of the sun. (Not bad for the same dufus who took 120,000 years to come up with a comb!)

Our ancestors do not seem to be *gradually* using tools, gradually developing language, or *gradually* using trial and error to build a few hundred flawed structures until they finally get it right. It does not seem to happen this way.

In an article in *Science*, the respected paleoanthropologist, Stanley Ambrose, aware of this anomaly, makes a pithy observation: "A mere 12,000 years separates the first bow and arrow from the International Space Station."[65]

Human culture bursts onstage and gives the impression of a qualitative leap forward more than any quantitative "creep" up some Jacobian ladder of development.

And the pyramid of Giza, after standing in the sun for 5,000 years, enduring floods, earthquakes, continental drift, and decomposition, still boasts that its north points north and its south south with an *inaccuracy* of only 0.06 percent.[66]

The pyramid which our idiot-savant builds will stand as tallest stone building on earth *for the next 43 centuries*, surpassed only by 18th century construction. And not to forget, our ancestor-eggheads built an almost identical set of structures on another pyramid plane far off in China at roughly the same time.

Science writer Will Hart expresses the dilemma another way:

> . . . We are still fumbling around trying to understand the mysteries of the pyramid cultures of prehistory, and of how we made the quantum leap from the Stone Age to civilization in the first place! It does not add up . . .
>
> As they had little to no experience with wild grains, how did they know what to do to process them, or even that they were indeed edible . . . How did Stone Age man suddenly acquire the skills to domesticate plants and animals and do it with a high degree of effectiveness? We find purebred dog species like salukis and greyhounds in Egyptian and Sumerian art: How were they bred so quickly from wolves.
>
> The Sumerians were making bread and beer five thousand years ago and yet their very close ancestor . .knew nothing of these things and lived by picking plants and killing wild beasts. It is almost as if they were given a set of instructions by someone who had already developed these things.
>
> . . . Circa 8000-5500 BC, the tribes in the Nile Valley were living in semi-subterranean oval houses roofed with mud and sticks. They made simple pottery and used stone axes and flint arrow-

heads. They were still semi-nomadic and moved seasonally from one camp to another. The vast majority of tribes around the globe were living in a similar state. How do we get from there to quarrying, dressing, and manipulating one-to sixty-tone stones into the world's most massive structure, and in such a short time? .. where are the smaller-scale pyramids . . . much smaller? Where are the crude stone carvings that precede the sophisticated stelae? The slow evolution of forms, from simple to complex, is all that human beings knew, not mud and thatch-roof huts and then large scale architecture employing megalithic blocks of stone.

. . . the developmental phases are simply not there . . . The problem is that there is no intermediate step between them and Sumeria and Egypt . . . The orthodox theories are starting to rely more on the "official pronouncements" of authorities rather than on well-argued and well-documented facts.

We have reached a crisis in the field of anthropology, history and archeology, because the conventional theses are unable to solve an increasing large number of anomalies. The explanations are thin and threadbare and . . . unable to support their own weight. The pieces do not lock together and fit into a smooth coherent whole.[67]

Curiously both our Egyptian and Chinese pyramid builders *insist* they got their inspiration, their skills, and knowledge from extraterrestrial ancestors and forefathers, Osiris in the case of the Egyptians, and the 'Sons of heaven' in the case of China. Sumerians attributed their civilization to visitations by the Gods Enlil, Enki, and their cohorts. And, as we documented in chapter three, they are quite specific in saying that knowledge of medicine, surgery, mathematics, and the domestication of plants and animals came from their "Gods."[68]

Mainstream cultural anthropologists retort:

Oh no you didn't! We're still looking for an explanation, but we're quite sure you didn't get anything from the Gods. Your myths, epistles, cuneiform tablets, cylinder seals, and all those other recitals are just superstitious, deluded logorrhea. We'll get back to you when we've figured it out. Maybe it was agriculture and the recession of the ice age; maybe mutated frontal lobes, maybe non-zero sum meme acceleration, but we can tell you now, definitively and unambiguously, none of your achievements came from extraterrestrial sources. No gods were here, and none gave us anything, no writing, no commandments on tablets, no math, no science, no pyramid plans, no blueprints, no secrets of metallurgy . . . nothing . . . We discovered all of that, through trial and error and plodding gradualness. Sorry to disappoint!

If the explanation is to be found in the human genome, those genes took an awfully long time to express themselves after 124,000 years of dormancy. To reiterate: Neanderthal's cranial capacity is *larger* than ours, and he was here close to 200,000 years, but never invented a wheel, any written language, any agriculture, or any kind of counting system by the time of his extinction. [69]

With our superior cognitive debut on this planet, we matched our retarded cousin's dullardry doltishly walking hand-in-hand for at least 120,000 of those years—maybe even 186,000 years— before showing any genuine signs of brilliance and inventiveness.[70]

So is it not problematic to anchor the florescence of *Homo sapiens* culture to a *gradual* evolution of the human genome?

The changes in our capacities are far too immediate to pull out that plum. We have to postulate a storm of mutations in an extremely short span of geological time that Darwin would barely have time to put on his rain coat.

The weird thing in all this discussion is that *he actually wrote to us about his transformation!*

He left us messages on walls. He buried papyri in caves. He gave us the *Pyramid Texts*, the *Nihongi*, Hesiod's *Theogony*, *The Epic of Gilgamesh*, the Indian *Rig Veda*, and *Mahabarata*, the Japanese *Kojiki*, the Mayan *Popol Vuh*, the Babylonian *Enuma Elis*, the *Turin Papyrus*, [71] the *Tibetan Book of the Dead*, the *Aztec Song of the Dead*, Ethiopia's *Kebra Nagast*, the Persian *Shahnameh*[72] and the Sumerian cylinder seals. Indeed almost all of *Homo sapiens*'s earliest writing dealt with this theme.

I'm not talking about creationism here, a banal, naive, and crypto-conservative view of man's origin—and this book is not an attempt to rationalize any such accounting. To the contrary, *Homo sapiens* commentary on the subject of our extraterrestrial contacts is found in the oral and written records of *virtually every culture on this planet*, Egyptian, Greek, Japanese, Judeo-Christian, Mayan, and Chinese sources. From

Zeus to Kronos, Dionysus, Krishna, Marduk, Xbalanque, Osiris, Viracocha, and Christ, the narrative of our ancestors coming from the heavens, or our being children of the Gods—or their apprentices—is ubiquitous.

So while present scientific biases teach that we should treat this archaic literature as superstitious *Homo sapiens* graffiti, I have one singularly politically incorrect suggestion: Those forefathers who putatively mated with us, or inserted a few snippets of DNA into our genome — or tutored us—and bequeathed moral codes, knowledge, written language, and cognitive precocity . . . . maybe it is just possible they came from elsewhere.

Virtually all our mythology says that is exactly what happened. Hypothetically . . . tentatively . . . guardedly . . . cautiously . . . *why not at least think about taking them at their word?*

How terrible would it be if a handful—just a handful— of evolutionary biologists, archeologists, and anthropologists actually studied this hypothesis, legitimately *within* academia rather than outside it? Why must it be so egregious to suggest that our apocalyptic rise out of 124,000 years of stone age-stupor into the brilliant beings that created the seven wonders of the world as rapidly as we did might, just might have been influenced by outside agitators?

Why should this hypothesis be treated as occult fantasy? Perhaps because it is confused with evangelical creationism, and, if so, that is indeed unfortunate.

Academic Political Correctness

When you search academic databases for 'human extraterrestrial origins,' you find no articles at all. I do not know of any academics presently studying the issue of whether the *Homo sapiens* genome may have had an extraterrestrial influence. Such papers are entirely nonexistent in anthropology and archeology databases.

On Google, if one punches in "alien hybrid" there are 2.4 million hits, and if you use "mankind extraterrestrial origin" you get another three million, but in both the anthropology and archeological databases, there are *fewer than ten articles*, and all of these deal *solely* with geological evidence for extraterrestrial meteors.

Galileo

We only need recall the problems of Nikolaus Copernicus, Johannes Kepler, Galileo—and even Sigmund Freud—to remind ourselves that simply putting a hypothesis on the table can cost a person their reputation. And in some cases more than that.

Giordano Bruno said the universe was boundless, that stars were suns, and that the rotating earth revolved about the Sun. For his heresy Bruno was held in prison eight years and finally burned at the stake by the Inquisition in 1600. (It took the Vatican 400 years to absolve him of his "crimes".)[73]

Giordano Bruno

In these days of lingering political correctness, we have to admit science sometimes is shackled and bound to an agenda that places many ideas, like the one we are pursuing in this chapter, *totally* outside its margins.

Two Modern Examples: Immanuel Velikovsky

Trained as a psychoanalyst, and believing that myth and dreams contained important clues about *real* things, Immanuel Velikovsky found a mother lode of insight in ancient manuscripts. His extensive studies of Egyptology and other cultural texts led him to suggest the earth's history was far more catastrophic than the uniformitarianism contemporary science suggested.

He wrote of this in his first major work, a bestseller, entitled *Worlds in Collision*.

Throughout his career he made a number of uncanny and prescient empirical predictions, yet all were all aggressively ridiculed by the establishment.

For example, he said that Venus ought to be hot because mythic literature often referred to this sacred body as incandescent. He supposed that a large comet once collided with earth. He suggested that cometary tails contained hydrocarbons, and that Jupiter emitted radio noises. As these predictions were put forward, none were considered meritorious.[74] Velikovsky was treated as a quack, accused of "delusions of grandeur," and relentlessly condemned, with astronomer Carl Sagan often leading the pack. "Velikovsky was systematically attacked in the scientific journals . . . while there never seemed to be a space in which he could reply in order to defend himself,"[75] says one commentator.

Immanuel Velikovsky

Despite the fact that *World's in Collision* was a best seller, the scientific community got into such an uproar over its publication that the editor at Macmillan who accepted his work, and who had worked for Macmillan for twenty-five years, was sacked.

As time marched on, however, establishment science had to wipe a considerable amount of egg off its face. In the 1950s astronomers said held that Venus was freezing cold and only an incompetent like Velikovsky could hold otherwise. But in 1962, NASA's Mariner II satellite showed Venus was scorching hot and reached 1000 degrees Fahrenheit.

Later it was shown that a comet did, in fact, catastrophically impact earth, that cometary tails indeed possessed hydrocarbons, and that Jupiter most certainly emitted radio waves, all predictions made many years earlier.

Clearly his most fearful suggestion was that the Earth might have been a party to these ancient planetary upheavals. This was his most grievous sin against the establishment, and the psychological crux for accusations against him.

Computers simply were not capable enough of running scenarios of planetary orbits over millions of years in those days to see if slight perturbations of one orbit—Venus or Mercury for example—could result in planetary collisions. But in 2009 a large-scale study by Jacques Laskar of the Paris Observatory ran "computer model (which) accounts for gravitational interactions among the moon, the eight major planets, and Pluto, including the effects of general relativity. The team ran simulations up to five billion years. The result: . . . Mercury collides with Venus in about 1.7 billion years; Mars swings within 800 kilometers of Earth . . . and in 196 simulations, "Earth was struck 48 times; once by Mercury, 18 times by Venus and 29 times by Mars." [76]

Velikovsky has been gone for over 30 years, but were he alive to hear these findings, we'd probably hear an "I-told-you-so," under his breath.

John Mack

John E. Mack was a tenured professor of psychiatry at Harvard Medical School with scores of publications and a pristine reputation, even a Pulitzer Prize. A group of debunkers, who wanted to expose those they thought to be hucksters—people who said they had been abducted by aliens, came to Professor Mack for his assistance. Dr. Mack was one of America's leading experts in clinical hypnosis.

Harvard Professor and Pulitzer Prize recipient John Mack

They asked this prestigious professor to put these subjects in a trance and expose them as mentally unstable crackpots. Mack was no UFO buff (or skeptic, for that matter), but he thought the enterprise sounded fascinating. He took on the project as an ally of the skeptics, but after hypnotizing numerous abductees, he observed none had any observable psychopathology, and most seemed to repeat the same story, trance after trance, with an uncanny concordance in detail under deep hypnosis.

He wrote of his astonishment in *Abduction: Human Encounters with Aliens* and suggested, cautiously and respectfully, that it was *possible* these people actually might be reporting real experiences.

> I have never encountered anything similar to this in patients I
> have known to be traumatized by humans, or in psychotic pa-
> tients suffering from delusions . . . It's a complicated, consistent
> narrative that operates clinically altogether like a real experi-
> ence. [77]

Despite his tenure, prior distinguished publications, and profes-
sorship, Harvard absolutely crucified him. A university committee was
formed to examine his credentials, and then to reexamine them. The
inquisition from on-going, multiple university investigations lasted
over fourteen years. His teaching, his prior publications, his personal
life were all meticulously scrutinized. Mack spent $100,000 of his own
funds on attorneys to defend himself against allegations of "validating
the delusions of his patients." Shortly before Mack's recent and un-
timely death—he was killed by a drunk driver— he confided to a friend
that he felt the only way he could get his reputation back would be to
act like Galileo and "recant." To the best of my knowledge, he never did.

Clearly there are political and ideological forces slithering through
the academy which are suppressive, restrictive, and highly lethal to
one's career.

Personal Sidebar

In the case of this text, one valiant research microbiologist kindly
reviewed the biological section of this chapter for accuracy. I wanted
to make sure that none of the speculations I was proffering here were
too far out, or if my sources or data could be considered suspect. She
answered quite emphatically, "No!" That was reassuring.

When I asked her how the extraterrestrial hypothesis might be experimentally tested. She said "if extraterrestrial contact had a mutagenic influence, ancient DNA samples would look significantly different
from DNA sampled today." (This was actually hinted at in our Mungo
Man discussion.) I then asked her whether I could cite her as a source,
but she demurred and said I should simply refer to her generically as a
"research genetic anthropologist."

So my "anonymous" external reviewer privately thought the hypothesis was reasonable and even had empirically testable edges, but

for reasons of her career and reputation she sought to remain anonymous. This is the ethos in which this idea is tendered. The hypothesis
that species *Homo sapiens* might have been schooled or genetically altered by extraterrestrial contact regrettably *is found nowhere in serious
academic discussion.* [78]

As Murray Gell-Mann, the quantum physicist who discovered the
quark—and obviously speaking from experience— reflected: "Most
challenges to scientific orthodoxy are wrong . . . A lot of them are crank,
but it happens from time to time that a challenge to scientific orthodoxy is actually right. And the people who make that challenge face a
terrible situation." [79] I'm sure Professor Mack would concur.

Conclusion

So this biological conjecture, our fourth chapter, is perhaps our
most speculative enterprise. In our first four chapters, we tried to
merely present all the empirical evidence that would be suggestive of
alien contact from archeology, mythology, the paranormal, and finally
this biological perspective.

In our next and final chapter we will see if our databases fuse and
synthesize, whether they present some kind of composite picture
which is persuasive of extraterrestrial contact, or whether, to the contrary, we should put our speculative tails between our legs and hum-
bly return to the standard model that we are indeed "just an advanced
breed of monkeys on a minor planet of a very average star." [80]

That mainstream model would remind—and, in fact, admonish—
us that our peculiar ancient edifices and pyramids are explainable
merely as outcroppings of indigenous cultures which built them, that
our mythologies little more than delusory wish-fulfillments and fables,
that paranormal UFO "witnesses" are deeply tainted by hallucinations,
misperceptions, conspiracy theories, and overzealousness, that crop-
circles are practical jokes, and our biological conjectures meaningless,
anti-Darwinian twaddle.

So let us begin the debate and look at all the evidence gathered so
far to see if this standard model is indeed the true one, or if there really
is something to any of this.

> *It is better to debate a question without settling it than to*
> *settle a question without debating it.*—*Joseph Joubert*

Doing to others what they did to you?

> *US researchers have genetically modified mice to be better at*
> *learning and remembering. Team leader Joe Tsien, a neurobiologist at*
> *Princeton University said simply: "They're smarter."… The research*
> *team from Princeton, Washington and MIT universities found that*
> *adding a single gene to mice significantly boosted the animals' ability to*
> *solve maze tasks, learn from objects and sounds in their environment and*
> *to retain that knowledge… It is the blueprint for a protein that spans the*
> *surface of neurons and serves as a docking point, or receptor, for certain*
> *chemical signals. This receptor, called NMDA, is like a double lock on a*
> *door; it needs two keys or events before it opens…*
> *Humans also have the added gene, although it is not yet known*
> *whether it has the same function in people.*
> *This new strain of mice is named Doogie, after a precocious*
> *character on the US television show Doogie Howser, MD.*
> —*"Genetic engineering boost intelligence." BBC News Sept 1, 1999*

Endnotes

1 Karl Abraham, *On Character and Libido Development*. New York: W.W. Norton, 1966 p.66

2 http://en.wikipedia.org/wiki/Ring_a_Ring_o%27_Roses

3 Note: this flu actually originated in the United States but came to be known as the Spanish flu.

4 Vana G, Westover KM (June 2008). "Origin of the 1918 Spanish influenza virus: a comparative genomic analysis". *Molecular Phylogenetics and Evolution* 47 (3): 1100–10.

5 Photo source:http://interconnections.co.uk./Health/Kurlian

6 Thelma Moss, *The Body Electric*, New York: Jeremy P. Tarcher Inc., 1979.

7 Michael Talbot. *The Holographic Universe. Ibid.*

8 Gods, Genes, & Consciousness, *Ibid.*, p. 262.

9 F. David Peat, *Synchronicity: The Bridge Between Matter and Mind*. New York, Bantam, 1987, p. 190.

10 Paul Von Ward, *Gods, Genes and Consciousness, Ibid.*, p. 23

11 Gods, Genes, and Consciousness, *Ibid.*, p. 300.

12 W Raymond Drake, *Gods and Spacemen of the Ancient Past.* New York: New American Library, 1974, p. 98.

13 "DNA sleuths redraw path of human development." *San Jose Mercury News,* July 11, 1997, p. 22A.

14 *Ibid.*

15 That is to say, out of 378 nucleotides of DNA examined, Neanderthal mitochondrial DNA differed from that of humans and chimpanzees in 27 places. Human DNA is 98.4% identical to the DNA of chimps and bonobos. Orangutans, gorillas, chimps and bonobos all were left-brained while monkeys were not. "See Monkeying around with the brain. *San Francisco Chronicle,* May 11, 1998, p. A2.

16 Neanderthals make big splash in gene pool. *Science News.* Vol. 152. July 19, 1997p. 37.

17 "DNA Sleuths," *Ibid.* p. 22A.

18 Suplee, *Ibid.*

19 Neanderthal linked to man debunked." *San Francisco Chronicle,* March 29, 2000, p. A8.

20 John Wilford. "Europeans could be part Neanderthal," *San Jose Mercury News,* April 25, 1999, p. 4A. See also "Neanderthals show staying power in Europe." *Science News,* Vol. 156, p. 277 October, 1999. A final study reports that the oldest Neanderthal DNA discovered as about 40,000 years old. However, a 100,000-year-old Neanderthal tooth recently provided DNA. The authors concluded, "The Neanderthal sequences exhibit chemical arrangements not observed in people, supporting the theory that Neanderthals produced no or few offspring with our ancient forerunners." See "Variety spices up Neanderthals' DNA." *Science News,* June 16, 2006, p. 381.

21 A German study is underway to decipher the Neanderthal genome. Nicholas Wade "Scientists hope to unravel Neanderthal DNA and human mysteries." *New York Times,* July 21, 2006.

22 Tina Hesman Saey, Team decodes Neanderthal DNA, *Science News,* March 14, 2009, p. 6.

23 Others suggest the age of Homo sapiens is 150,000 years. Lewin, Roger. *New Scientist.* 19 July 1997: 5.

24 Out of Africa vs. Multiregionalism December 7, 1999 source: stevenjaygould.org

25 Conroy, G. *Reconstructing Human Origins: a Modern Synthesis.* (W.W. Norton & Company: New York, New York & London, England) 1997 p. 439-440

26 Leakey, R. "Early Homo sapiens remains from the Omo River region of south-west Ethiopia: Faunal remains from the Omo Valley" *Nature* 222(1969):1132-1133

27 Malcolm Ritter, "Ethiopian fossils dated to 195,000 years, called oldest remains of modern humans." Associated Press, *The Miami Herald* International Edition, Feb. 17, 2005, p. 10A. In addition "Fossils of early Homo sapiens previously discovered in 1967 in the Kibish region along the Ethiopian Omo River have now been redated to about 195,000 years ago by a team of American and Australian scientists including

Ian McDougall, Francis Brown, and John Fleagle. According to the latest research results published by McDougall et al. (2005) in *Nature*, "both skulls probably stem from chronologically comparable silty sapropel layers of the so-called Member I of the Kibish Formation. Their find levels are now dated to about 195,000 years by a tuff layer positioned slightly below the fossils and providing a terminus post quem of 196,000 years on basis of its content of radioactive Argon." Source: *Athena Review*, "Archeology in the News," http://www.athenapub.com/archnew2.htm

28 "Human fossils are oldest yet." *Science News*. Feb., 26, 2005, Vol. 167, p. 141.

29 A recent piece in *Science News* may push our age as far back as 250,000 years. See Tina Hesman Saey, "First rough draft of Neanderthal genome released." *Science News*, March 14, 2009. Another unique study of mitochondrial DNA of the Sandawe people in Tanzania showed modern humans to be 170,000 years of age. Source: Ann Gibbons, *Science*; 6/13/2003, Vol. 300 Issue 5626, p1641

30 Will Hart, *The Genesis Race*, Rochester Vt: Bear & Co., 2003, p. 27; Note that since the human chimpanzee genome has not been deciphered, one wonders how this figure was estimated.

31 It has been recently argued that some 1500 human genes appear to contain unique mutations compared to chimps. Source. Human genes take evolutionary turns, Jan. 17, 2004, *Science News*, p. 165.

32 I shared the "alien hybrid" hypothesis with a Harvard academician, Dr. Maryellen Ruvolo, a professor in Harvard's Anthropology Laboratory. Her comments, by no means validating the idea, were at least generous enough not to pooh-pooh it outright. Most interesting in our exchange of emails was that now that the human genome has been deciphered, scientists are rapidly on the way to deciphering the chimpanzee genome. Once this is accomplished, we should have a better idea of exactly which genes are distinctly human and divergent from chimp DNA. Presently we are only guessing at the level of differences between human and chimp, but the research base is steadily growing. Since this email exchange, decoding the chimpanzee DNA has been rapid and is described further in this chapter. (Note that Dr. Ruvolo is not the genetic research anthropologist cited later who reviewed the biological section and sought to remain anonymous.)

33 Randolph E. Schmid, "Study tightens chimp-human link," *San Francisco Chronicle*, May 20, 2003, p. A2.

34 Britten, R.J. 2002. "Divergence between samples of chimpanzee and human DNA sequences is 5% counting indels." Proceedings National Academy Science 99:13633-13635.

35 Leigh Dayton, N.Y. *Times Syndicate*, cited in *The News*, Mexico City, Jan. 15, 2001, p. 20.

36 Tiffany Mayer, *Ibid.*, May 15, 2001

37 http://www.convictcreations.com/aborigines/prehistory.htm

38 Ian Tattersall & Jeffrey Schwartz, *Extinct Humans*. Westview Publishers, 2000.

39 "Branchless evolution." *Science News*, April 15, 2006, p. 227.

40 Gene, fossil data back inverse human roots, *Science News*, Vol. 159, Jan. 13, 2001, p. 21.

41 Originally thought to be 62,000 years old . . . "The consensus was unanimous—Mungo Man was buried about 42,000 years ago," says geologist Jim Bowler of the University of Melbourne who discovered Mungo Man in 1974 in the dry bed of Lake Mungo in New South Wales. Mungo Man is the oldest ritually buried skeleton in the world—his body was painted with ocher.

42 A study conducted by the Gibraltar Museum reports Neanderthals may have been alive in Spain as recently at 24,000 years ago. Malcolm Ritter, "Study: Neanderthals lived later than thought." Associated Press, September 14, 2006.

43 From West's Serpent in the Sky. See http://en.wikipedia.org/wiki/Egyptian_pyramid_construction_techniques

44 A very recent study once again corroborates that there is a difference of approximately 1.44 percent between chump and human DNA sequences. Science News, June 12, 1004, Vol 165, p. 382.

45 Carl Sagan, The Dragons of Eden, New York: Random House, 1977, p. 4.

46 Cro-Magnon is a term which falls outside the usual naming conventions for early humans and is used to describe the oldest modern people in Europe.

47 Robert Wright. Non-Zero: The Logic of Human Destiny. New York: Random House, 2000.

48 A very recent study asserts that evidence for agriculture; specifically the cultivation of wild grasses along with grains and cereals can be pushed back to about 23,000 years ago. See "Seeds of agriculture move back in time," Science News, July 24, 2004, vol. 166, p. 61.

49 Another problem in this argument is that in Giza, where the great pyramid was built, agriculture was not established in 10,000 BC, nor even by 7000 BC. There is no evidence of firmly established agriculture until 5000 BC, a thousand years after its appearance southwestern Asia, and quite late to be able to create a dense, highly populated region where the greatest edifice on earth would suddenly spring up. Source: Christine Hobson, The World of the Pharaohs, Ibid., p. 49. In addition Wright assumes memes like agriculture spread culturally and through learning, but recent evidence suggests that the spread of agriculture from early farmers in the Middle East into Europe was a function of gene transmission and intermarriage. "Farming spread into Europe via population mixing rather than by natives simply adopting agriculture." See "European face-off for early farmers." Science News, January 7, 2006, p. 14.

50 Bruce Bower, "Brain Size Surprise: All primates may share expanded frontal cortex." Science News, March 13, 2004; Vol. 165, No. 11 , p. 163

51 Randolph E. Schmid, "Study tightens chimp-human link," San Francisco Chronicle, May 20, 2003, p. A2.

52 Robert Wright, Ibid., p. 287.

53 Recent studies of gorillas in northern Congo have also been found to use tools (a branch to test the depth of a river) to the surprise of investigators. See "Wild gorillas take time for tool use." Science News Oct 15, 2005, Vol. 168

54 Sources for the domestication of horses come from Bruce Bower, "The Botai of central Asia milked marks more than 5,000 years ago." *Science News*, March 28, 2009.

55 Table based on dating anatomically modern Homo sapiens at 130,000 years.

56 Table adapted from data provided in Jared Diamond, *Guns, Germs and Steel*. New York: Norton, 1999. See also "Early farmers took time to tame wheat." *Science News*, April 15, 2006, p. 237.

57 Parker, S. 1992. *The Dawn of Man*. Crescent Books.

58 "Neanderthals take out their small blades." *Science News*, May 13, 2006, p. 302.

59 Strausbaugh L. and Sakelarisc, S. 2001 "DNA and Early Human History. Neanderthals and Early Humans: But Did They Mate?" Univ. of Connecticut. Presented at the Evolution Symposium, NABT Convention, Montreal 7 Nov. 2001.

60 Will Hart, *Ibid.*, p. 148.

61 Will Hart, *Ibid.*, p. 74.

62 Z. Stitchin, 1980 *The Stairway to Heaven* Avon Books, New York, p. 86.

63 http://myweb.tiscali.co.uk/davel/The%20Great%20Pyramid.htm

64 Marshall Payn, "The Case for Advanced Technology in the Great Pyramid," *Forbidden History, Ibid.*, p. 270.

65 Cited in http://www.usatoday.com/news/science/aaas/2001-03-01-tooluse-evolution.htm

66 The first exhaustive survey of the monument in modern times was carried out by Sir Flinders Petrie in 1880-2. He used the latest equipment of the time and approached his task with great thoroughness. He found that the sides of the pyramid were indeed lined up almost exactly with the cardinal points of the compass: north, south, east and west. (The accuracy of this alignment is incredible, with an average discrepancy of only about three minutes of arc in any direction; this is a variation of less than 0.06 per cent.) Source: http://fusionanomaly.net/greatpyramidsofgiza.html.

67 Will Hart, "Ancient Agriculture: in search of the missing links." *Forbidden History*, Douglas Kenyon (ed)., Vermont: Bear & Co, 2009, p. 200–201

68 Zacharia Sitchin, *The 12th Planet*. Rochester, Vt: Bear and Co, 2002.

69 Gore, R. & Blair J. "1989 Extinctions." *National Geographic*, June 1989.

70 If one uses the 196,000 Omo skulls as the first date of anatomically modern Homo Sapiens, then the last 10,000 years of cultural advancement would occur after 186,000 years.

71 The Turin Papyrus, now in the Egyptian Museum in Turin, states that the first rulers of Egypt were the gods themselves, followed by demigods and finally the people it called "the followers of Horus." Christine Hobson, *The World of the Pharaohs*, London: The Paul Press, 1987, p.22

72 Andrew Collins. *From the Ashes of Angels*. New York: Bear & Co., 2001, p. 116. See also p. 35 for the *Kebra Nagast*.

73 W. Raymond Drake, *Gods and Spacemen of the Ancient Past*, *Ibid.*, p. 26.

74 John Kettler, "The Martyrdom of Immanuel Velikovsky," *Forbidden History*, *Ibid.*, pp 53-68.

75 Ketter, *Ibid.*, p. 57.

76 Sid Perkins, "Gravity's influences could mean bumpy ride for inner solar system." Science News, July 4, 2009.

77 Cited in Lynne Kitei, *The Phoenix Lights*, *Ibid.*, p.144.

78 If there is any "alternate hypothesis" to try to explain the sudden emergence of human culture in so short a time, it might be attributed to the growth of agriculture. Beginning between 10,000-7000 BC, the spread of agriculture liberates people from the toils of hunting and gathering, allows greater division of labor, creates the groundwork for the establishment of cities, so the rise of written languages, technology, mathematics, etc., might be explained away by the discovery by homo sapiens of how to domesticate plants and animals.

79 Tom Siegfried. "The status quark." Sept 12, 2009, *Science News*, p. 24.

80 Quote attributed to physicist Stephen Hawking.

7. Could It Be True?

*Man cannot discover new oceans unless he has
the courage to lose sight of the shore.*
—Andre Gide

Before we try to sift and sort our databases and formulate an answer to our question, let us review our museum tour of this topic.

The Archeology Room

Our first excursion took us into strange territory. We encountered Egyptian hieroglyphs that looked like they were depicting flying machines. We turned up a 5,000-year-old sycamore glider stuffed in a dusty box showing ancient Egyptians knew something about aerodynamics. We came upon Sumerian referents to a nine-planet solar system, an insight which, if true, was 4,500 years premature.

Moving from one exhibit to the next, we were taken by ancient Japanese sculptures of creatures that appeared to be dressed in space suits. We found a text showing Saturn's rings long before modern telescopes ever observed them. We logged a few virtual hours in Africa with the Dogon who worshipped an invisible star near Sirius half a millennium before it was ever seen with a telescope. We dug up a map of Antarctica—actually two—which had an uncanny correspondence to recent radar imaging of the continent. To have such an accurate correspondence with images taken of mountainous areas and river valleys long hidden under massive ice sheets, such maps had to be drawn prior to 4,000 BC when the area might have been ice-free.

Things started getting curiouser and curiouser.

We took our magnifying glasses and examined the Voynich manuscript, which has eluded all efforts to decipher it, including the most sophisticated cryptographic decoding programs in our arsenal. So far, the text seems to bear no correspondence to any human language past or present.

And, then we examined the incredible array of stone cutting technology that spanned the globe, from the largest hewn rock ever produced by our species, the stone of Baalbek, to the Pyramids of the Giza plane, and the incredible structures in Sacsayhuaman and Puma Punktu where at least one granite rock showed evidence of machining to within a 50th of an inch of tolerance.[1]

Certainly one of the most amazing exhibits was the uncanny alignment of three ancient and disparate structures which appear to point to the major stars in the belt of Orion: the pyramids of Giza, remarkably similar alignments of the Chinese White Pyramid plane, and the recent discovery in England of the Thornborough henge. What makes this perplexing is that the Giza plane was designed and engineered between 2,600 BC and 3,000 BC, the Thornborough henge between 3,500- 2,500 BC, and the Chinese White Pyramid plane about 3,000 BC.[2] We know [f]rom conventional history no single society was in all three of those places at that time, and there weren't any shuttles either.

One conclusion from the archeological room alone was that none of these exhibits *directly* pointed to alien intelligence or alien intervention. Perhaps indirectly yes, but there are some other reasons which could explain away much of this data, like some unknown precursor culture. We will get to that soon, but first let's continue our museum redux.

The Mythology Room

Here we uncovered to our surprise far stronger evidence of extraterrestrial contact: an absolutely ubiquitous written testimony about beings, gods, and machines coming from the heavens and returning.

Unless we attribute all this evidence to wish fulfillment, hallucination, and human delusion, we have to begrudgingly consider this written record "moderately strong." The evidence of entities coming from afar and returning in ships of various size, type, and hue goes from Ezekiel to the Eskimos. We listed sixty-one sky-gods who are described in mankind's earliest writings from the Japanese *Nihongi* to the Persian *Shahnameh*, and dozens of ancient texts betwixt and between. [3]

The Paranormal Room

As we entered the first of our two paranormal rooms, we marveled at the UFO exhibit. This evidence is really the only "direct" evidence we encountered for extraterrestrials. These are not inferences from archeological digs, nor interpretations of ancient manuscripts, but myriad eyewitness accounts, most of which have been reported since the nuclear age began. Maybe those reports started flowing in because we were collectively becoming more superstitious and irrational—or maybe those two thousand atmospheric tests of nuclear weapons between 1945 and 1963—by the U.S., France, England, and Russia—attracted some outside interest. [4]

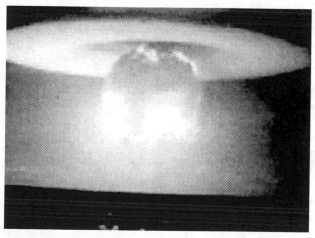

Atmospheric H-bomb explosion

When we reviewed this data, reviewed the validity of astronaut's claims and efforts to debunk them, our conclusion was that the evidence was certainly persuasive, but, at the same time, not definitive.

Consider this statement by noted scientist, Michio Kaku, author of *Quantum Field Theory: A Modern Introduction.*

> In my mind, there is no question they're out there. My career is well established. My textbooks are required reading in all the major capitals on planet earth. If you want to become a physicist to learn about the unified field theory, you read my books. Therefore, I'm in a position to say: Yes — Most likely they're out there, perhaps even visited, perhaps on our moon.[5]

We listened carefully to scientific and insider devotees, but also heard from debunkers and skeptics and were surprised how many notable accounts could be dismissed as fictitious, uncorroborated, sheer rumor, or misquoted pieces of data. Still, they couldn't all be dismissed, and many respected and informed souls remain. This is certainly an area receiving the highest marks with respect to our journey and our question.

Our next paranormal room contained crop circles. While crop circles were elegant and sophisticated, they are highly subject to fraud. Interesting data has been accumulated which makes it more difficult to disregard them out-of-hand as the productions of vandals equipped with boards and PVC pipe. Persuasive studies recorded unusual magnetism inside, strange mineral deposits, signs of burning and radiation, anomalies in bent crops growth patterns, and peculiar germination rates which make the out-for-a-laugh hypothesis more than dubious. Still, I found it difficult to follow this thesis to its ultimate end, particularly the conclusions one might draw from the study of the pixelled crop circle in Chilbolton.

Even though it may be difficult to embrace this data for some, it is even more difficult to dismiss it. First, even skeptics must admit that one undiscovered Euclidian theorem was encoded in a group of these figures and published in a peer-reviewed journal by a distinguished mainstream astronomer-academician who successfully decoded them. What kind of "conspiracy of vandals" produced over fifteen separate crop circles expressing a Euclidian theorem never before known or published?

If entirely human in origin, why not come out of the shadows—stop already with the crop circles!—and publish your stunning and exquisite mathematical discovery in a reputable journal?

A second showed an uncanny pictograph of *pi* out to ten decimals and similarly published in a prestigious journal. That alone makes the subject of crop circles deserving of scientific interest and far less ridicule.

Finally, since there are over 10,000 recorded crop circles and only about seventy people ever caught making them, it seems they had to be made it furtively. Is it really possible to say that *all of them* are coming from nerdy, intelligent, math majors armed with PVC pipe and eye-hand coordination so thoroughly advanced that such incredibly articulate and precise constructions all could be laid out and crafted under the cover of darkness by beer-drinking pranksters?

The Biology Room

There was one remaining exhibit, biological evidence for possible extraterrestrial intervention that might offer to explain the inexplicably laconic appearance of human culture.

Our other hominid cousins, Neanderthal and *Homo erectus* in particular, do not antedate us with gawky machines, wheels that cumbrously spin, or butterfingered settlements made out of the wrong kind of mortar. They just don't seem to possess these kinds of artifacts, edifices, languages, drawings, or tools. Neither did we for the longest time, and then suddenly we did. Bang! Big Bang!

Specifically, Neanderthal wandered the northern reaches of our planet for 170 millennia, and we explored its surface for a good 120 with nary a hint of intellectual precocity. Neither of us. That's a total combined period of mutual, shared, cognitive sluggishness of 300,000 years—and still neither came up with a bow and arrow, no one thought of domesticating a wild pig, nobody thought up a phonetic alphabet—even though recent genetic evidence suggests Neanderthal also was equipped for speech—and neither species seemed smart enough to consider cultivating a potato.

If we were to ask what exactly *Homo sapiens* was doing which was superior to *Homo Erectus* or Neanderthal during all this time, we would be hard pressed to list any real behavioral differences. A recent *Scientific American* article makes clear that it is entirely indeterminate if *Homo erectus*, Neanderthal, or *Homo sapiens* was smarter or more ingenious than the other.[6]

If brain size, tool use, language development, and cognitive capacity are going to be explained by evolutionary theory, it is necessary to postulate rather apocalyptic mutations in our DNA *suddenly*, and in the very, very recent past. Even 24,000 years ago, we find a cave in Europe's Iberian coast, which both Neanderthal and *Homo Sapiens* shared, and differentiating the two with respect to tool use or *any differential cognitive sophistication* is entirely indeterminate.[7]

Beginning only about 8,500–7500 BC[8] *finally* there are signs of animal and plant domestication and organized settlements, but it is really not until about 4,000 BC that human culture absolutely explodes. Beginning after the fourth millennium with the advent of the Sumerian and Egyptian civilizations to the present, a mere 6,000 year period, human cultural advancement exponentially accelerates.[9]

Physical anthropology insists that this human cultural eruption has to be explained by biology and genetics in some way. One way is to say that a mysterious set of rapid mutations gave us cognitive capacities much greater than Neanderthal, such as larger or more complex frontal lobes. Not only was our brain smaller than Neanderthal, but research cited earlier shows that there is no substantial or significant *qualitative divergence* in frontal lobe development in comparison to a number of other primate species. Sigh!

A second rationale is based on the end of the ice age. The mainstream argument goes like this: With the recession of the ice-age comes farming. With farming, populations are no longer nomadic, and sedentary peoples create increasingly complex divisions of labor: populations increase, cities form, writing and technology develop. But if agriculture was the ultimate cause for the ascent in human culture, as radical environmental determinists suggest,[10] we are puzzled.

If you look at a map of the last ice age at its maximum,[11] there were plenty of areas still available to develop agriculture. Why didn't we?

Why did it take agriculture so long to even start up in the first place (at least 122 millennia from our inception as a species).[12]

Secondly, if agriculture creates sedentary populations which, in turn, boost divisions of labor and intellectual achievement, why did great and flourishing agriculturally-based, sedentary civilizations, like the Inca Empire which stretched 2,500 miles across the continent of South America as late as AD 1200, still never develop writing?[13]

The cultivation of maize has been pushed back to as early as 2,000 BC in Peru,[14] and yet even three thousand years later, no writing system appears. If the society was citified, sedentary, and unburdened from daily drudgery, where was the poetry and literature? The Incas reached their zenith *forty centuries after* the Egyptians proudly mused over their hieroglyphs and the haughty Sumerians polished their cuneiform tablets, but those Inca bookshelves were still empty.

The step-by-step gradualness of cultural evolution seems to skip quite a few steps, if not trip and stumble along its explanatory path.

Connecting the Dots

The flowering of human culture from its pyramids to this interconnected planet, begins—let's be honest—not much earlier than 8,000 BC. For a species that is at least 130,000 years old, the tardiness is staggering and suggests that something qualitatively striking occurred to alter us so much in so little time.

There was a "great leap forward," from phlegmatic stone-age intellectual simpleton to an innovative, literate, pyramid-building genius . . . a metamorphosis that happened, frankly, in a Darwinian nanosecond.

To say it another way—and perhaps more precisely—if we date the vast majority of human cultural evolution as occurring in the last 12,000 years as paleoanthropologist, Stanley Ambrose[15] said, and we use for our benchmark the latest research for the first appearance of anatomically modern *Homo sapiens* as 196,000 years (recall the Omo skulls), then our cultural emergence only truly *begins* in the 94th percentile of our time on this earth.

Prior to that we were as doltish as our simian and hominid relatives. Only in the most recent six percent of our time here has our anatomically modern species shown significant evidence of a gathering intellectual ability. This sudden ascent is nettlesome if it is to be explained by a gradual, developmental, evolutionary set of changes occurring *within* our species in this tiny sliver of time.

While modern anthropology at least has the courage to admit that it is perplexed by the furious ascent of human culture, it is curious that our mythological record is so blatantly ignored.

Physicists and astronomers don't ignore it. They have no difficulty consulting ancient books to fix the date and time of a supernova or to identify the dates of various earthquakes or droughts. In fact one Sumerian cuneiform tablet accurately describes Halley's comet.[16] The physical sciences routinely use mythology as a reliable and accurate repository of human archaic memory, but when it comes to the issue of human origins, anthropology insists any such evidence is, of necessity, irrational, hallucinatory, and superstitious regardless of how prolific or cross-cultural.

Mythology is treated like a little elementary school child made to sit in the back of the room wearing a dunce's cap and admonished to "stay quiet." The message from our ancient literature has been rendered mute; the point of view it espouses is completely and thoroughly brushed aside.

But ignored, shunned, and sitting with a frown under that dunce's cap there is still a quiet voice murmuring. And that voice says that humankind has been influenced and changed as a result of visitations from outer space by Gods, beings, creatures, vessels, spirits, angels, and in sundry other entities from Ezekiel's space ships to the vessels that carried the pharaoh off with 33 other divine beings. Sure, there is a lot of diversity in these accountings, from one language to the next, one people to the next, and one epoch to the next, but the common underbelly of these mythological narratives is that we have been designed, educated, altered, *and/or* are the actual offspring of extraterrestrial interactions.

From Zeus to Kronos, Dionysus to Krishna, Osiris to Christ, the *Pyramid texts* to Hesiod's *Theogony*, the testimony that our species is the product of hybridization or tutelage from heavenly beings is ubiquitous.

But anthropology demands that we ignore the misfit in the back of the room under the dunce's cap and premise everything man has done on evolution, DNA, and the human genome *without recourse to any outside intervention.*[17]

To evolutionary geneticist Dean Hammer:

> The original humans' lifestyle was not terribly different from that of the Neanderthals. They were primarily hunters and gatherers. Then something changed. *Within an eye blink of geological time,* and for reasons that anthropologists still don't understand, man blossomed. Humans began to talk to one another. They began to paint and sculpt, to sing and dance. Soon they were farming and building permanent residences.[18]

The neurological complexity of dolphins is very close to *Homo sapiens* with respect to the ratio of brain size to body mass; its frontal lobes are similar—its cortex 40 percent larger[19]—yet in all the years that dolphins have been swimming around, close to 50 million years, we never discovered a dolphin settlement, city-state, underwater monument, religious temple, or any ongoing experiments in aqua-technology.[20] They do manage to pick up a sponge and use it as a tool in Australia to protect their sensitive snouts while foraging, but so far this is the only "culturally transmitted tool-use" ever observed from our neurologically sophisticated water-brothers.[21]

Beyond our inability to explain the breakneck rise of human culture premised on recent and massive still-unknown changes in the *Homo sapiens* genome, there are other problems to explain.

We need to understand how the very first pyramids in Egypt were not of the stumbling, bumbling, one-of-these-days-were-going-to-get-it-right variety, but the first ones turn out to be some of the most incredible engineering achievements in the history of the human race, *far superior to any of the pyramids that followed!*

It isn't supposed to work that way.

We don't start out with a BMW 750i and gradually evolve to a Honda Civic and then end the evolutionary progression with the glorious Edsel.

But with pyramids that is what seems to happen. The most spectacular human construction, the Great pyramid of Giza, (Cheops) turns out to be superior to virtually all the pyramids built *afterward.* And these latter edifices were not improvements in structural engineering, but generally crumbling, ersatz, wanna-be imitations.

Inside the Great Pyramid is a sarcophagus made out of a solid piece of granite. Its measurements shows an interior volume of 1166.4 and an exterior volume of 2332.8 liters, a ratio of external to internal volume that is *exactly* twice measured to the precision of a tenth of a liter. There is no indication that Egyptian craftsman possessed any equipment which would have allowed this kind of precision. As for the cutting of the sarcophagus . . .

> . . . it must have been cut either with bronze saws studded with diamonds or saws of a much harder metal. But diamonds have never been found in Egypt, and at the same time the sarcophagus was supposedly made, metals harder than bronze were unknown to the Egyptians or anybody else on earth.[22]

Indeed one researcher took some modern tools, accurate to one one-thousandth of an inch, and tried them out on that sarcophagus.

> Their smooth, flat surfaces, orthogonal perfection, and incredibly small inside corner radii that I have inspected with modern precision straightedges, squares, and radius gauges leave me in awe. Even though after contacting four precision granite manufacturers I could not find one who could replicate their perfection.[23]

So when we apply an evolutionary perspective to all of this, as if our brains, capacities, technologies and culture *gradually and progressively* improve over time, our hard drives freeze. With the Egyptians, nothing seems to happen the way it should.

Researcher and scholar Peter Tomkins writes about the Great Pyramid as follows:

Till recently there was no proof that the inhabitants of Egypt of five thousand years ago were capable of the precise astronomical calculations and mathematical solutions required to locate, orient, and build the pyramid where it stands. It was attributed to chance that the foundations were almost perfectly oriented to true north, that its structure incorporated a value for *pi* accurate to several decimals and in several distinct and unmistakable ways; that is main chamber incorporated the "sacred" triangles . . . which were to make Pythagoras famous, and which Plato in his *Timaeus* claimed as the building blocks of the cosmos. Chance was said to be responsible for the fact that angles and slopes display an advanced understanding of trigonometric values, that its shape quite precisely incorporate s the fundamental proportion for the "Golden Section," known today by the Greek letter *phi* . . . . According to modern academicians the first rough use of *pi* in Egypt was not till about 1700 BC—at least a millennium *after* the Pyramid; Pythagoras' theorem is attributed to the fifth century B.C.; and the development of trigonometry to Hipparchus in the second century before Christ . . . Recent studies of ancient Egyptian hieroglyphs . . . have established that an advanced science did flourish in the Middle East at least three thousand years before Christ, and that Pythagoras, Eratosthenes, Hipparchus and other Greeks reputed to have originated mathematics on this planet merely picked up fragments of an ancient science evolved by remote and unknown predecessors.

Whoever built the Great Pyramid, it is now quite clear, knew the precise circumference of the planet, and the length of the year to several decimals—data which were not rediscovered till the seventeenth century. Its architects may well have known the mean length of the earth's orbit round the sun, the specific density of the planet, the 26,000 year cycle of the equinoxes, the acceleration of gravity, and the speed of light.[24]

Either some unknown, highly advanced, lost civilization antedated the time of the Great Pyramid, or the human cultural big bang is just too apocalyptic, sudden, and amazing to be attributed to a local, terrestrial, gradual evolution of cognitive abilities and technologies.

Not only did the culture that built the pyramids have the math and physics, incredible stone carving techniques, and an uncanny sense of the cardinal points of the earth in its construction, but their language,

Egyptian hieroglyphs, appeared just as suddenly without any lengthy period of proto-hieroglyphics preceding it and with few developmental precursors.[25] According to Jared Diamond:

> Hieroglyphic writing appeared rather suddenly, in nearly full-blown form, around 3000 BC. Egypt lay only 800 miles west of Sumer, with which Egypt had trade contacts. I find it suspicious that no evidence of a gradual development of hieroglyphs has come down to us, even though Egypt's dry climate would have been favorable for preserving earlier experiments in writing.[26]

Beyond Jared Diamond, other scholars similarly conclude that Egyptian hieroglyphs and Sumerian cuneiform, which appeared a century or two before, are entirely different from each other with neither influencing nor evolving one from the other.[27]

Make a mental note of the gaping and obvious problem in our mainstream logic: Modern anthropology would tell us that it takes 124 millennia of anatomically modern *Homo sapiens* dimwittedness before the species finally gets the idea of domesticating a horse—*that's 1240 centuries*—but the time it takes from the very first appearance of Egyptian written language to the building of the Great Pyramid, which cuts, moves, and fits the largest blocks of stone on earth in ways that today we cannot even duplicate, *that* only takes only six centuries!

It is incomprehensible to reconcile that these structures and their monumental technology were built in a culture that between 400-600 years earlier *had no written language and, no symbolic mathematics*.[28] In other words, only 4-600 years pass from the first appearance of hieroglyphic writing to the construction of the Great Pyramid, but it takes over 120,000 years from our beginnings as a species before we first get the idea of domesticating a goat. As TV cynic John Stossel, would say, "Gimme a break!"

Something strange happened to us that seems *enormously* atypical and certainly not a gradual, developmental, progressive, unfolding of inventions, technologies, or "memes.

An Alternate Point of View

The Precursor Culture which Explains Away Our Data

There are non-extraterrestrial theories that might give this data a fair shot at an alternate hearing. In the interest of fairness, let's try one on for size. Here is a contrarian point of view, a composite of the work of Immanuel Velikovsky, Graham Hancock, Charles Hapgood, and, would you believe, Albert Einstein. [29]

Due to the weight of ice sheets covering the earth and their melting during deglaciation, the crust of planet earth actually shifted rapidly in one swift, jerky movement. Suddenly Siberia, which was covered in grasses, froze overnight, and mammoths were freeze-dried for thousands of years with undigested grasses in their stomachs. Sounds strange, I know, but a lot of important data fits.

> The remains of mammoths are found all around the Arctic Circle with food still in their mouths and stomachs that indicates that they were grazing in a temperate climate when they died . . . Siberia was warm at the time, and it suggests that not only must the death of the animals have been sudden, but the bodies must have cooled very rapidly, or these delicate plants would have been dissolved in their stomach acid. It is thought that a cooling to -150 degrees Fahrenheit, from a starting temperature of around + 80 degrees, would have been necessary to stop the digestion process in time. [30]

Can you imagine the earth cooling at such a rapid rate? Einstein thought the hypothesis of a sudden shift in the earth's crust was an attractive one. He even consulted with Hapgood about the hypothesis, and their association led to a 170 page to-and-fro correspondence. [31]

Not only would this explain how mammoth stomach contents remained undigested, but it also offers us an idea about how tropical vegetation could be found in Antarctica.

So, one day, under the giant ice sheets of Antarctica or Greenland we might find remnants of a lost civilization, perhaps the Atlantis of Plato, which perhaps turned to ice as quickly as the mammoths of Siberia. Maybe then we shall uncover a more ancient cultural past and fill in the enormous gaps so that many of the oddities we have discovered can then fit into a revised, albeit *conventional*, chronology.

So if we hypothesize something like Atlantis existed, and this lost culture influenced the building of pyramids in China *and* Egypt, explored the earth, developed a sophisticated mathematics, and was skilled in geology, metallurgy, and engineering to create incredible rock-cutting and quarrying technologies that can be found in such disparate locales as Egypt, Baalbek, Peru, and Bolivia, then we would have a credible hypothesis to compete with the extraterrestrial one.

And if mythical Atlantis existed, say, between 14,000 BC and 10,000 BC, we would be able to see human culture and civilization developing far more modestly, millennium after millennium, and our perplexities would be calmed. Things would be moving far more gradually.[32]

Such a prototype or precursor civilization which went the way of the mammoths and was destroyed in a massive cataclysm like a shifting of the earth's crust, could be a reasonable inference and one that would explain away much of the archeological evidence we have been discussing. *Still*, the notion is premised upon two *enormous* speculations (1) that the earth's crust shifted in a sudden planetary shock, and (2) that such an advanced culture not only existed, but also succumbed to the disaster.

While those speculations might seem attractive, the real issue here is why such a hypothesis isn't considered just as *outrageous* as the extraterrestrial one?

If our mythological record can be taken seriously, it wasn't Atlantis that was responsible for our precocity. It was that we encountered other advanced beings who taught us, led us, and/or through marriage or genetic tinkering, altered our DNA to make us what we are—children of another kind of ancestor.

We learned from 42,000 year old *Homo sapiens* Mungo Man that his DNA was *vastly different* from our present structure. And his is the earliest known anatomically modern *Homo sapiens* DNA from which we could get a viable extraction. It does not conform to what we expected.

Is it possible that we may have taken on snippets from elsewhere since the time of Mungo Man, and those shreds of DNA account for the rapid, unexplained and exponential rise in human capacity, culture, language, and technology?

Curious New Genes

Dr. Jonathan Pritchard from the University of Chicago reported recent results of a genetic study called "The Hap Project." Researchers identified 700 regions of the human genome where genes appear to have been shaped "within the last 5,000 to 15,000 years," and some of these genes appear related to cognitive functioning.[33]

Reporting in *Science*, Bruce Lahn and his colleagues at the University of Chicago identified two genes which have gone under substantial evolution in the last 37,000 years, one having to do with brain size, and an "ASPM variant" of that gene arising some 5,800 years ago and now found in roughly 30 percent of the species.[34]

A third line of recent research isolated the *HAR1* gene, differing from chimp DNA by only 2 out of 118 base pairs, and this also seems to be a recently evolved gene that could be related to reasoning and learning.[35]

Explaining our delayed cultural advance will probably take on the character of proposing these kinds of recent genetic alterations like *HAR1* or *ASPM*.[36] Together these discoveries could represent the 'smoking gun' for *Homo sapiens* exponential cultural emergence, the springboard from which human culture jumps after its long period of dawdling.

Certainly it is possible these modifications evinced themselves in a manner entirely governed by the process of natural selection, but mutagenic changes usually take eons more evolutionary time. Recall that it took roughly 1.5 million years for the *Homo erectus* cranium of about 1000 cc to evolve into our 1350 cc skull,[37] —and not to forget Carl Sagan's discussion of the 100,000 years it took to morph into a human big toe. To have seven hundred modifications in the human genome—plus others occurring so very recently—raises an eyebrow. Is it possible they occurred as a result of outside interaction or intercourse with the beings our mythologies have rhapsodized?

Ashur, one of the Sumerian's pantheon of sky Gods

The ancient Egyptians told us where the hieroglyphs came from. They didn't come from Atlantis. They didn't come from trial and error. They didn't come from a millennium of gradually improving doodles. They came from the gods, from the sky. They were *imported.* They called their hieroglyphs *mdju netjer* . . . "words of the gods."

Ditto for the Chinese who identified the source and builders of their White Pyramid complex not from any mariners of Atlantis, nor from a millennia of piling up dirt with little buckets until someone stood up and said "Gosh, we've got a pyramid here!" No, they credit their gigantic mound and its celestial alignment to their *ancestors from the sky.*

And they footnote the development of agriculture and medicinal herbs to their "divine farmer," Shennong, another sky god. [38]

But it is *de rigueur* in anthropology to dismiss that testimony as occult fantasy.

Bragging Rights

On their elaborate tablets and steles, the Sumerians might have told us of their long, enduring, and frustrating developmental struggles to create that advanced system of weights and measures, how they painstakingly cultivated botanical domesticates generation after generation, or how they spent a few centuries perfecting the very first musical instruments.

Just as we inscribe our elementary school books with the names of Edison, Eli Whitney, and Henry Ford, how proper if the Sumerians and Egyptians gave credit where credit was due. How helpful if they serenaded us and celebrated the names of all their great inventors and developers, in metallurgy, shipbuilding, musical transcription, and ceramics, *but they didn't.*

None of these cultures wrote of themselves in this manner.

The Egyptians tell us explicitly that their knowledge came from the stars. Why should we reflexively throw out that testimony without a shred of doubt that they might have been tying to tell us something?

From far Antiquity the Egyptians believed that Osiris and Isis descended from the skies to bring a wondrous civilization to the Lands of the Nile . . . The Book of the Dead vividly described the Shining Ones from the stars . . . after great cataclysms the Gods returned to those glittering constellations bejeweling the night leaving their descendants, the God-King, to govern Egypt.[39]

The Sumerians referenced their gods Enlil, Enki, and other sky gods for their knowledge and advances in agriculture,

> Without Enlil, the great mountain, no cities would be built, no settlements founded. No stalls would be built, no sheepfold established. No king would be raised, no high priest born.[40]

> From all these accountings—Greek, Sumerian, Chinese, Mesoamerican, Egyptian, Japanese, Persian, Indian—*Homo Sapiens* either is an alien hybrid or the heir to a few centuries of tutelage. Today any tenure-track anthropology professor who thought of taking that hypothesis seriously would be gingerly escorted out of the ivory tower in a heartbeat. Simply not going to happen.

The Symbolism of the Sphinx

Oedipus is asked to solve the riddle of the Sphinx. "What walks on four legs in the morning, two legs at noon, and three legs in the evening?" He answers "Man!" Man crawls on all fours in infancy, walks upright on two legs in adulthood, and uses a cane in old age. Riddle solved.

The riddle of the Sphinx, so attractive to Freud and the ancient Greeks, is solved by the assertion that *the Sphinx is a structure that represents Man.*

While Oedipus was looking at a different sphinx entirely in 350 BC, Jung alerted us to interpret symbols by sometimes just looking at them and asking what we see.

Well, the Sphinx currently dated to about the same time as the Great Pyramid, is, to this day, the most maximalist sculpture on earth over thirteen stories tall and a city-block long. And what does it depict? What do we see?

It shows us the head of a man or god attached to the body of a beast. Perhaps that is exactly what the ancients wanted to memorialize. The "beast" here is one *Homo sapiens* pinhead indistinguishable from Neanderthal in intellectual dexterity. He had something attached to him, however, a head, a divine nature, an astonishing intellectual capacity that metamorphosed and transformed a hunter-gatherer half-wit into the most awesome reigning species on earth.

The Sphinx is a hybrid. Jesus himself is a hybrid, half man, half god. Just as so many ancient Greek heroes were the offspring of the Immortals, is the riddle of the sphinx saying the same thing about us . . . *and to us?*

Archetypes, Genes, and Hard Wiring

If *Homo sapiens* is some kind of alien hybrid, do we have any more proof for this kind of speculation? Actually no, not directly, but Harvard geneticist Dean Hammer says he found something peculiar: *Homo sapiens* spiritual sense, his tendency to look towards the stars and the Gods, might actually be a genetically based.

For a psychological trait to be considered genetically rooted, it must pass through a rigorous methodological filter. Take homosexuality as an example. When data is obtained on the frequency of adult homosexuality in pairs of identical twins and then *compared to the frequency of that trait in fraternal twins*, whenever a statistically significant discrepancy occurs, the most reasonable explanation for the divergence falls at the feet of the *genetic invariance* shared by identical twins, but not fraternal.

Using this methodology, homosexuality, for example, has been shown to possess a 'heritability' factor of 0.50, meaning its occurrence can be explained as roughly 50 percent nature and 50 percent nurture. "Obesity" and "criminality" also passed through the identical-fraternal twin filter, and both are considered partially genetically based, albeit possessing lower heritability scores.

Using the procedure with the reliably measured, psychometric trait of "spirituality," Hammer finds its heritability almost as high as homosexuality or 0.43. That is to say the spiritual sense in our species appears to be an *inherited predisposition.*[41]

> The correlation for identical twins was .37, about double the correlation of .20 for fraternal twins. When these numbers were analyzed, the estimate for heritability came out to 43 percent. In other words, nearly half of the reason the twins felt religion helped them, spent time privately praying, and had a sense of God's presence, was inherited. Since these twins were raised by different parents, in different neighborhoods, and sometimes even in different religions, their similarities seemed to be the result of their DNA rather than their environment.

If spirituality is a genetically based, inherited predisposition, then one might easily pose the following dilemma: if religious belief is delusional and absurdly magical, how and why did it get into the genome?

Ever-skeptical evolutionary biologist, Richard Dawkins, refers to religion as "a virus of the mind . . . (from) a parasitic group of myths and falsehoods that serve no biological function or advantage."[42] If the *Homo sapiens'* propensity toward religious belief is really the expression of a maladaptive and aberrant genetic mutation, what adaptive purpose could such a mutation have served all this time?

Homo sapiens seems to be genetically hardwired to look to the stars. Furthermore, the species has been busily engaging a vast and extensive repertoire of rituals and practices to that end, millennium after millennium, while its other neurologically evolved planetary companions, Neanderthal, *Homo erectus*, dolphins, great apes, and bonobos do not appear similarly oriented at all.

Is it possible the Gods not only have been delivering aphorisms, parables, caveats, and moral codes *verbally* on tablets and scrolls from umpteen mountain tops, but also etch-a-sketching on the human genome and grafting a divine imprint in a way not possessed by other creatures on earth?

Curiously even in the Bible, there is a cryptic reference to such hard-wiring in which God has inscribed his code and "written in their hearts." Romans 2:13-15 John Calvin called it *sensus divinitatis*, a "sense of deity inscribed in the hearts of all."[43] Herodotus said the same in 350 BC. Ditto for virtually all primitive cultures, which seem to possess religious mythologies—and cognitive imprints— pointing to the stars.

In an earlier chapter we poured over a long list sky gods who interacted with man, but we could add into this mix all the ancient creation myths that, in one variant or another, describe how creatures from the heavens created man. Not all cultures possess such myths that look up to the heavens, *but the majority does.*[44] The following table lists quite a few more.

There are two ways to think about this discussion. One is to consider the *Homo Sapiens* archetypal religious fixation as an aberrant genetic mutation that has caused our species to adhere to a delusional and magical set of maladaptive beliefs which are mysteriously fully resistant to the corrective surgery of natural selection *for eons and eons* or, to the contrary—that the Gods left a genetic footprint in the form of a archetype.

As Carl Jung said about God—or the gods—they have . . .

> . . . made an inconceivably sublime and mysteriously contradictory image . . . without the help of man, and implanted in man's unconscious as an archetype . . . not in order that theologians of all times and places should be at one another's throats, but in order that the unpresumptuous man might glimpse an image, in the stillness of his soul, that is akin to him and is wrought of his own psychic substance. This image contains everything he will ever imagine concerning his gods or concerning the ground of his psyche.

Table 7.1 Cultures with Creation Myths Pointing to the Heavens

Ainu	Dyah	Kagba	Nyamwezi
Algonquin	Efik Ekoi	Krachi	Pawnee
Altair	Fang	Lanoan	Popo
Arikan	Fulaini	Lugbara	Skagit
Assyrian	Hopi	Malozi	Society Isle
Bagobo	Hottentot	Mande	Swahili
Boshongo	Huron	Maori	Tahilian
Buriat	Ijaw	Minyong	Thonga
Celtic	Inca	Modoc	Wakaranga
Cheyenne	Iroquois	Mosetene	Wapangwa
Dhammai	Joshua	Nandi	Yoruba
Dogon	Indians	Negritos	
		Ngombe	
		Ngurunderi	

Conclusion and Synthesis

The quintessential idea of this text is that mankind's sense the gods and another world beyond this can be understood as a *memory trace*, preserved in myth, of contact with extraterrestrial civilizations which interacted with or even mated with our ancestors.

From mysterious space-suited Dogu statuary to the Voynich manuscript; diatonic encrypted crop circles; compelling and suppressed UFO reports; ancient precocity in pyramid building, cartography, and mathematics; mysterious African tribes worshipping an invisible companion star of Sirius 700 years before it was discovered; sudden appearances of full-blown written languages; pyramids scattered around the globe, almost identical pyramid planes in Egypt and China, and English "henges" . . . we assembled a mosaic of data that represents both direct and indirect empirical evidence that there may be more to this hypothesis than meets the eye.

From Baalbek to Sacsayhuaman to Puma Punkta, the evidence scavenged is speculative, no doubt, but it is not an idea to be impeached *merely* because of its political incorrectness.[45]

We have become far more intelligent than our simian brethren, not because we have a few more neurons than *Homo Erectus*, or because we have up to a five percent edge in DNA ahead of chimps, or even because agriculture developed allowing humanity to flourish *finally* after an insipid 122 millennia of hunting and food-gathering. Something *weird* happened in *very recent history*, and the dawdling gradualness of genetic and cultural evolution is conspicuously wanting in its accounting of the cultural paroxysm of the last 10,000 years.

That *Homo sapiens* is an alien hybrid, or perhaps the heir of an apprenticeship of extraterrestrial pedagogy, is a *competing hypothesis* that purports to account for our tempestuous cultural big bang.

Our origins are not merely of this world. They stretch back in time, to touch ancestors who were not merely our chimpanzee brothers and sisters but may implicate a progenitor *not of this planet*.

Perhaps mankind's need to feel important or wanted or free of death, pain, and misery, prompts those divine aspirations, and maybe that is why our mythologies were concocted in the first place. Who knows, maybe that is why we see so many UFOs in the sky as well.

But is it not curious that these heavenly notions and our star-studded bias seem to exist everywhere and for all ages past and present. More interestingly, we cannot find any such ideas in very similar creatures. Neanderthal, in 1700 centuries of nomadic wandering, did not appear to bury his dead for any religious purpose,[46] and never created a cathedral, much less an altar.[47] There are no *Homo erectus* sacrifices[48] to the gods of which we can be sure; and certainly no dolphin, bonobo, or orangutan behaviors betray any concern for a divinity or the heavens.

> Jane Goodall records how the death of an adult male chimp, who broke his neck falling out of a tree, led others to display intense excitement and anxiety around the corpse, even throwing stones at it . . . yet as close as chimps and other higher order primates are to us biologically, they appear not to indulge in any elaborated behavior towards the corpse which is simply discarded and left.[49]

Only our species, it seems, drags out the incense and the red ochre to paint its face with untold designs and tattoos to adorn a conspicuous symbolism that solemnizes a thousand after-death rituals, pointing to the stars, pointing to our ancestors from the sky, and pointing to life elsewhere. What makes matters worse, it manages to carry on these dances, sacraments, ceremonies, and spectacles virtually *everywhere on earth* and has engaged in such practices as far back in time as we can extrapolate.

The cult of the Caroline Islands built a memorial, a straw airplane, which was a replica of the plane that brought John Frum to them. Their rituals recapitulate and memorialize that event as they await the promise of their sky-god to return with more precious "cargo."

John Frum worshippers look to the heavens. Left, they have constructed a straw replica of his as they await the return their god's return.

Humankind does the same thing—and far earlier —constructing strange and unusual monuments all across this planet, tracing lines large enough to be visible deep in outer space, and worshipping gods who come from stars and star systems which are identified *as the source of his ancestral origin, as well as his destiny.*[50]

The Nazca lines of Peru. We know that these lines when seen from the air (photo to the right) depict creatures, birds, and are so large they can only be seen by flying above them in a plane. Recently, however, NASA released photos of other Nazca lines, significantly larger, which can be seen best not from airplanes but from outer space. These perfectly straight lines (left) are roughly 4 miles by 7 miles in length.

All this happens while his cousins, from chimps to Neanderthal, all with coextensive brain structures, almost identical DNA, and often transplantable organs, keep their noses to the ground, preen themselves, forage for food, and languish in their natural habitats blissfully intact without any acknowledgment of deities, divinities, or the vaguest superstitious interest in the stars.

Our rituals and myths often are ways of remembering, of memorializing important events in our collective history, whether it is a planetary flood—which myriad cultures report in their respective mythologies—or visitations from people of the sky.

Where Do You Stand?

You have to evaluate the evidence yourself and for yourself: to weigh mainstream science against these conjectures, to balance skeptics and debunker arguments against the interpretations of empirical evidence you have encountered between these pages.

Let us put some of this into a psychological focus. Look at the ratings on the attached table and scale. Why not rank them according to your own evaluations as, I have ranked mine:

In this text we left out Sasquatch, poltergeists, and other kooky, tabloid items of collective fascination. We tried to take on the most salient databases and examine the evidence.

Potential ratings	1	2	3	4	5	6	7	8
	Ridiculous		Speculative but interesting		Plausible & persuasive		Definitive	
Sources of evidence								
Archeological				X				
Mythological						X		
Reports of UFOs						X		
Crop circles			X					
Biological				X				

To complete this scale, rate each source of evidence on an 8-point scale and place a checkmark in the appropriate box a91, if you feel the evidence is "ridiculous" or 8 if you fell the evidence is "definitive." Total your scores for each source off evidence and divide by 5 to get your composite score. My composite score in the example above is 4.6.

If you decide it is all poppycock and ridiculous, then back you go to the halls of the academy to return to your intellectual pursuits unencumbered by any of these speculations. If, on the contrary, you feel the evidence is definitive, your next step, probably, is to join with the existing international organizations to lobby them, like astronaut Gordon Cooper did, so that evidence will not be suppressed by governments and bona fide inquiries begun by well-staffed, unbiased, and objective scientists. And if you decide, as I have, that the evidence is "plausible, but not definitive," then you will likely continue on your journey of curiosity and wonder.

A Postscript: "What if . . .?"

Before closing, I would like to take you on a guided fantasy. Imagine that all those voices the UFO literature likes to cite: Gorbachev, Woolsey, NASA astronauts, and scientists like Michio Kaku . . . that all these folks were right. Imagine Neil Armstrong breaks his silence and finally corroborates that he made that secret transmission to NASA from the moon about UFOs.

To sweeten the pot, imagine the current buzz in the UFO community that President Obama will break with tradition and finally disclose that government has known about UFOs for decades and that UFOs are real.[51]

Imagine all of that happens.

So put your critical voice away. Think about the implications. No more doubts, no more skepticism. It's all true, at least the UFO part of the story. *Pretend* . . . just for a second.

What is interesting is what would happen to the evaluation of the databases presented in this book if we made that assumption.

Myriad scholars who have debunked mythological descriptions of flying saucers and gods coming from the heavens as fable, fantasy, and delusion, would have just enough time to wipe the egg off their faces to get to work revising their sense of history and their understanding of ancient literature. They would scour dozens of archaic tomes and, for the first time, see them as eyewitness accounts of events that might have actually happened.

Mainstream archeologists and anthropologists who pooh-poohed the Orion Belt as a sophomoric explanation of pyramid design would flush and blush only long enough to begin a whole new set of inquiries into monuments, from Mexico to Baalbek, and to see in these planetary-wide monoliths, henges, pyramids, and mounds possible extraterrestrial influences.

Anthropologists would fall into a deep funk and seriously wonder about how solid their traditional explanations have been for how agriculture started on this planet. Was it, as ancient texts repeatedly tried to tell them, an idea brought by extraterrestrial tutors?

Mathematicians and physicists would swarm over every new crop circle and photograph it endlessly before it disappeared, working far into the night to decode whatever encrypted meanings—that is, "communications"— were there. And they might drag a few microbiologists along with them.

Linguists would realize that a flying saucer had crashed in Aurora, Texas, in 1897 where local people said they saw "hieroglyphic writing." They would recall similar reports from Roswell in 1947 where the craft was said to contain "hieroglyphic-like writing." They would note that the Teotihuacanos who built the Pyramid of the Sun in Mexico used a still-undeciphered hieroglyphic writing. And when they re-read Egyptian accounts that their hieroglyphs were imported "words of the Gods," we might witness a full-scale review of just how humans came to develop written language in the first place.

Religious scholars would begin major re-appraisals of their ecclesiastical literature and the implications extraterrestrial visits may have on their theology. [Strange as that may seem, the Vatican already started such a study in 2009.][52]

And certainly there would be heated political inquiries into decades of government censorship and secrecy. Hearings would commence. Documents would be released. Congressional committees would look into whether debunkers, cynics, and disinformation experts were somehow bankrolled by government sources all this time.

Professors from every discipline would jettison their fears about having their academic reputations sullied, or ruined, and would uninhibitedly, if not gleefully, stampede out the door to investigate topics previously ridiculed by snooty peer-reviewers.

And finally, what would happen to biology and genetics? There is an encrusted consortium vested in the "gradualness" of evolution. But the thought that our genome could have been "tweaked" along the way—and, indeed, recently—with added cognitive and linguistic snippets here and there, would we not witness a similar rush out the door? Genetics would scrutinize everything previously dismissed as "junk DNA" and pour over this alphabet soup for "extraterrestrial codes" which might have played a role to differentiate us so markedly from our simian brethren.

It would not simply be "Gosh! It's true! UFOs are real!" that came out of this, but our physical and social sciences would be shaken to their very foundations. Our history, religious texts, mythologies, linguistics, microbiology, genetics, politics, research agendas, and our encyclopedias all would go through serious reappraisal and revision.

Well, a fantasy is, after all, just that, a fantasy.

Until that day comes—if it ever does—live long and prosper!

It followed us during half of our orbit [roughly 30 minutes].
We observed it on the light side, and when we entered the shadow side,
it disappeared completely. It was an engineered structure, made from
some type of metal, approximately 40 meters long with inner hulls. The
object was narrow here and wider here, and inside there were openings.
Some places had projections like small wings. The object stayed very
close to us. We photographed it, and our photos showed it to be 23 to 28
meters away.

. . . We are not alone in the universe. I believe someone or
something of extraterrestrial origin has visited earth. 53

—Video interview with Cosmonaut Victor Afanasyev, who
logged over 540 days in space.

Endnotes

1 http://www.ancient-wisdom.co.uk/extremasonry.htm. See also David Lewis "Evolution vs. Creation: is the debate for real?" in Douglas Kenyon, Ed., *Forbidden History*, Vermont, Bear & Co, 2005, p. 19.

2 Dating the Chinese white pyramid complex is in controversy and could be anytime between AD 1200 and 3000 BC.

3 Andrew Collins. *From the Ashes of Angels.* New York: Bear & Co., 2001, p. 116. See also p. 35 for the *Kebra Nagast*.

4 Source: http://www.cddc.vt.edu/host/atomic/atmosphr/index.html

5 http://www.netscientia.com/ufo_quotes.html

6 "Ian Tattersall, "We are Not Alone," *Scientific American*, Dec. 1999, p. 56.

7 Neanderthal debate goes south. *Science News*, Sept 23, 2006, p. 170.

8 Jared Diamond, *Guns, Germs &Steel*, ibid., p. 329.

9 Recent investigations decoding Neanderthal DNA suggest they share 99.5% of their DNA with *H.Sapiens*, but investigators still do not believe any significant interbreeding occurred between such remarkably similar species. See "New DNA test yields Neanderthal clues, showing genome nearly identical to humans." *New York Times*, November 16, 2006, p. A10.

10 See Jared Diamond's *Guns Germs and Steel* (ibid.) as an example.

11 Courtesy of http://www.johnstonsarchive.net/spaceart/earthicemap.jpg

12 See also "Last Big Meltdown," Prendergast, Kate, *History Today*, 00182753, Aug 2007, Vol. 57, Issue 8

13 Indeed if agriculture precedes the development of writing, the development of agriculture in Peru dates to some 5,380 years ago, at the height of the Inca empire. Four millennia later writing had yet to appear. See "Gone with the flow," *Science News*, Nov. 12, 2005.

14 Ancient Andean maize makers. *Science News*, March 2, 3006, Vol. 169, p. 132.

15 Cited earlier in this chapter.

16 Source: http://www.crystalinks.com/cuneiformtablets.html

17 A 1991 Gallup poll found that only 9 percent of the American public hold the belief that evolution proceeded strictly and solely through natural forces. See Dembski & Kushiner, *ibid.*, p. 43.

18 Dean Hammer, *The God Gene*, New York: Doubleday, 2004, p. 202.

19 Comparison of Primate and Cetacean Mentality (May 1998). Cited in http://serendip.brynmawr.edu/bb/neuro/neuro98/202s98-paper3/Ball3.html

20 Carl Sagan, *The Dragons of Eden, ibid.*, p. 38.

21 "Sponge moms," *Science News*, June 11, 2005, Vol. 167.

22 Whitley Streiber, *The coming global superstorm*. New York: PocketStar Books, 1999, p.61.

23 Christopher Dunn, "Precision," in *Forbidden History, ibid.*, p. 255

24 Peter Tompkins. *Secrets of the Great Pyramid*, New York: Galad Books, 1971, pxiii-xiv.

25 The earliest known writing comes from Uruk about 3300 BC in Sumerian clay tablets. Hieroglyphs appear about this time too, quite different, elaborated, highly aesthetic, and in the view of many scholars without antecedents. Source of photo and text: http://www.usu.edu/anthro/origins_of_writing/hieroglyph_aesthetics/

26 Jared Diamond, *Guns, Germs & Steel, ibid.*, p. 232.

27 Lamberg-Karlovskyh, C and Sabloff, J., 1979. *Ancient Civilizations: The Near East and Mesoamerica*. The Benjamin/Cummings Publishing Co., Menlo Park, California. p. 134.

28 There is controversy about which was the first written language (3400 BC, near Luxor, to 3200 BC, the first hieroglyphs). Bone and ivory tags, pottery vessels, and clay seal impressions bearing hieroglyphs unearthed at Abydos, 300 miles south of Cairo, have been dated to between 3400 and 3200 BC, making them the oldest known examples of Egyptian writing. Source Larkin Mitchell, "Earliest Egyptian Glyphs", *Archeology* Vol. 52, No. 2, March, 1999. There is also controversy about the actual date of the Great Pyramid. Some say it was built in 2590 BC, others as early as 3200 BC. The figure cited above uses a consensus of when the Great Pyramid was built, 2850 BC, and a consensus of the first written language in 3400 BC.

29 http://en.wikipedia.org/wiki/Cataclysmic_pole_shift_hypothesis

30 Whitley Strieber, *ibid*, p. 78-79.

31 J. Douglas Kenyon, "Atlantis in Antarctica," in *Forbidden History, ibid.*, pp 158-164

32 If Atlantis and the wooly mammoth disappeared at the same time in a rapid shifting of the earth's crust, the date would be roughly 10,000 BC. See http://en.wikipedia.org/wiki/Woolly_mammoth.

33 Nicholas Wade "Still evolving, human genes tell new story." *New York Times*, March 7, 2006, p. A1.

34 Genes tied to recent brain evolution. *Science News*, Sept 24, 2005, Vol. 168, p. 206. Note that critics hold these new alleles do no confer any new cognitive advantages.

35 "Evolutions DNA differences." *Science News*, August 19, 2006, p. 117.

36 Unfortunately a June 2006 report suggests ASPM does not exert an influence on brain size. "Evolving genes may not size up brain." *Science News*, June 3, 2006, Vol. 169.p. 349.

37 Leakey, R. and Lewin, R., 1992. *Origins Reconsidered*, Abacus Books, London, pp. 58-64.

38 http://en.wikipedia.org/wiki/Shennong

39 W. Raymond Drake, *ibid.*, p. 183.

40 Kramer, S. N. *History begins at Sumer*. Philadelphia: University of Pennsylvania Press, 1989, p. 92. Curiously, recent work on the spread of agriculture out of this area reports that there were striking anatomical differences between the advanced farmers who migrated out of the Middle East and their European hunter-gatherer cousins. See "Cultivating Revolutions," *Science News*, Feb. 5, 2005, Vol. 167.

41 Hammer's study is based on a large sample of some 1388 subjects. Hammer has even suggested that VMAT2 gene is the specific gene in question. Quotation is from Hammer, *ibid.*, p. 144.

42 Hammer, *ibid.*, p. 146.

43 Cited in Ronald Nash. *Faith and Reason*, MI: Zondervan Publishing House, 198, p39 See also William Dembski and James Kushiner, *Signs of Intelligence*, Grand Rapids, MI: Brazos Press, 2004, p. 53.

44 David Leeming, *A Dictionary of Creation Myths*, New York: Oxford University Press, 1994. See also: *The Origin of Life and Death: African Creation Myths*: Ulli Beier (ed). London: Heinemann, 1966.

45 Compare it for a moment to superstring theory in modern physics. Superstring theory attempts, through ingenious mathematical formulations, to unite quantum mechanics, the physics of the very small, to general relativity, the physics of the very large. It does so by postulating over ten spacetime dimensions to unify myriad sets of equations. The mathematics may be elegant, but there is virtually no empirical support for the theory. According to science writer, Noboru Nakanish, physics suffers from "superstring theory syndrome," and "makes no experimentally verifiable predictions," Scientist Reiner Hedrich echoes that sentiment saying the theory has "fundamental problems with empirical test-

ability, problems that make questionable its status as a physical theory at all." Superstring theory is speculative, empirically wanting, and most certainly indirect, but it is immensely *popular*. It is the rage in physics departments, chic, aucourant, and a fresh Ph.D. seeking an academic appointment with such an approach in his background is an absolutely sought-after hire. In contrast, imagine the reaction of an anthropology search committee interviewing a recent Ph.D. for an appointment. The candidate says he feels significant and weighty evidence exists, from the Giza to Sumerian cuneiform tablets, suggesting extraterrestrial intervention in human affairs—even in human biology—and this is his major area of research interest. Well . . . Good luck . . . and goodbye! Popularity and political correctness have substantial influence in academic decision-making, but the empirical support for the extraterrestrial hypothesis, controversial as it may appear, is a far cry *more visible and palpable* than all the cumulative experimental evidence supporting superstring theory despite the chichi character of the latter.

46 Iain Davidson, at the University of New England, is emphatic: "Modern humans were—and Neanderthals were not—deliberately buried." That cultural difference reflects a cognitive sophistication in one group of people unmatched in the other, he says. Source: Evolving in Their Graves. Ben Harder, *Science News*, 12/15/2001, Vol. 160, Issue 24.

47 There is some debate concerning whether Neanderthal had a religious sense. In one gravesite, circa 80,000 BC, Neanderthal skeletons were found neatly placed in fetal positions decorated with flowers, jewelry and tools, indicating perhaps a sense of an afterlife journey. Other Neanderthal gravesites, however, show scattered and gnawed bones suggesting Neanderthal practiced cannibalism and was casual with the bones of his brethren. Despite this anthropological debate any significant or momentous religious artifacts simply have not been found. Source: http://faculty.rpcs.org/reillyl/Neanderthal_handout.htm. Another study reports that of 200 Neanderthal skeletons, only 30 showed some rudimentary signs that mortuary or burial practices might be in evidence. Source: Mike Pearson, *The Archeology of Death and Burial, ibid.*

48 Although there have been no religious artifacts associated with homo Erectus, some anthropologists argue that Erectus did make engravings in bone, perhaps decorative, and that some symbolic life might be argued to belong to this early homo species. Alexander Marshack, "On Paleolithic Ochre and the Early Uses of Color and Symbol," *Current Anthropology*, 22:2, April 1981, p. 188

49 Mike Pearson. *The Archeology of Death and Burial.* Texas A & M U Press, 1999, p. 148.

50 Although a large number of ancient mythologies from all continents have creation myths which point to an extraterrestrial intervention or beginning, there are many which do not and which treat man's origin as coming from a cosmic egg, spirits from the underworld, the Raven, the Serpent, etc. See Creation Myths.

51 Curiously, President Obama in January, 2010 issued a new declassification memo-
   randum noting that secrets cannot be held indefinitely, and that all secrets
   more than 50 years old must be justified again in writing and approved by the
   President. Source: http://ww4report.com/node/8151

52 Barney Porter "Alien life is possible: Vatican." ABC News, Nov. 13, 2009. http://
   www.abc.net.au/news/stories/2009/11/13/2742484.htm.

53 Video interview entitled "Cosmonaut Victor Afanasyev;" see "astronaut" page at
   http://www.exopoliticsohio.us/ Afanasyev's biography is found at http://www.
   gctc.ru/eng/biogr/default.htm He is currently deputy director of the Yu.A.
   Gagarin Cosmonaut Research and Training Center.

SELECTED BIBLIOGRAPHY

Abraham, Karl. *On Character and Libido Development.* New York: W.W. Norton, 1966.

Bauval, R. & Gilbert, A. *The Orion Mystery.* New York: Crown, 1994.

Beier, Ulli. (ed). *The Origin of Life and Death: African Creation Myths.* London: Heinmann, 1966.

Childress, David. *Technology of the Gods.* Kempton, Illinois: Adventures Unlimited Press, 2000.

Collins, Andrew. *From the Ashes of Angels.* New York: Bear & Co., 2001.

Collins, Andrew. *The New Circlemakers.* Virginia Beach: 4th Dimension Press, 2009.

Conroy, G. *Reconstructing Human Origins: a Modern Synthesis.* New York: W.W. Norton & Company, 1997.

Corso, P. *The Day after Roswell,* Pocket Books, 1997.

Dembski, William and Kushiner, James. *Signs of Intelligence,* Grand Rapids, MI: Brazos Press, 2004.

Diamond, Jared. *Guns, Germs & Steel,* NY: Norton, 2005.

D'Imperio, M.E. *Voynich Manuscript an Elegant Enigma.* An Elegant Enigma 1981.

Drake, W. Raymond. *Gods and Spacemen in the Ancient East.* New York, New American Library, 1973.

Feats and Wisdom of the Ancients: Time-Life, Alexandria, Virginia, 1990.

Fernandez-Baca, Carlos. *Tupayachi. Saqsaywaman: A Model of Atlantis*, 2006, Biblioteca Nacional del Peru

Freudhen, Peter. *Book of the Eskimos*, London, 1962.

Gardiner, Sir Alan, *Egypt of the Pharaohs*, London: Oxford University Press, 1978.

Goldstone, Lawrence & Nancy. *The Friar and the Cipher*, New York: Doubleday, 2005.

Good, Timothy. *Need to Know*. New York: Pegasus Books, 2007.

Greer, Steven. *Extraterrestrial Contact: The Evidence and Implications*. Afton, VA: Crossing Point, 1999.

Griffin, Joseph. *The Origin of Dreams: How and Why We Evolved to Dream*, 1997.

Hammer, Dean. *The God Gene*, New York: Doubleday, 2004

Hancock, Graham. *Fingerprints of the Gods*, New York: Three Rivers Press

Hart, Will. *The Genesis Race*. Rochester VT: Bear & Co., 2003.

Haselhoff, Eltjo. *Crop Circles: Scientific Research & Urban Legends*, Berkeley, CA: North Atlantic Books, 2001.

Heinberg, Richard. *Memories and Visions of Paradise*. IL: Quest Books, Dec. 1994.

Hobson, Christine. *The World of the Pharaohs*, London: The Paul Press, 1987.

Kitei, Lynne. *The Phoenix Lights*, Charlottesville, VA: Hampton Roads Publishing, 2000.

Kosimo, Peter. *Not of this World*. The Clarendon Press, 1969

Kramer, S. N. *History Begins at Sumer*. Philadelphia: University of Pennsylvania Press, 1989.

Lamberg-Karlovskyh, C and Sabloff, J. *Ancient Civilizations: The Near East and Mesoamerica*. Menlo Park, California: The Benjamin/Cummings Publishing Co., 1979.

Lambert, W.G. & Millard, A.R., *Atrahasis, The Babylonian Flood Story and the Sumerian Flood Story*. Oxford: The Clarendon Press, 1969.

Leakey, R. and Lewin, R. *Origins Reconsidered*, London: Abacus Books, 1992.

Leenig, David. *A Dictionary of Creation Myths*, New York: Oxford University Press, 1994.

Marrs, Jim. *Alien Agenda*, New York: Harper Collins, 1997.

Matthews, Rupert. *Alien Encounters*. New Jersey, Chartwell Books, 2008.

McAndrew, J. *The Roswell Report: Case Closed*. Washington: U.S. Government Printing Office, 1997.

Moss, Thelma. *The Body Electric*. New York: Jeremy P. Tarcher Inc., 1979.

Nash, Ronald. *Faith and Reason*, MI: Zondervan Publishing House, 1989.

Parker, S. *The Dawn of Man*. New York: Crescent Books, 1992.

Pearson. Mike. *The Archeology of Death and Burial*. Texas A & M University Press, 1999.

Peat, F. David. *Synchronicity: The Bridge Between Matter and Mind*. New York: Bantam, 1987.

Podtrap Chandra, Roy. *The Mahabharata*, Calcutta, 1891.

Sagan, Carl. *The Dragons of Eden*. New York: Random House, 1977

Saler, B., Ziegler, C. & Moore, C. *UFO Crash at Roswell: The Genesis of a Modern Myth*: Washington: Smithsonian Institution Press, 1997.

Schopfung, Baumann. *Hermann Schöpfung und Urzeit des Menschen. Mythos der Afrikanischen Volker*, Berlin, 1936.

Silva, Freddy. *Secrets in the fields*, Charlottesville, VA: Hampton Roads Publishing, 2002

Sime, John H. "Embalming E.T." *Funerals of the Famous II*. New Jersey: Kates-Boylston Publishers, Vol. 2. 1996.

Sitchin, Zacharia. *The 12th Planet*. Rochester, VT: Bear and Co, 2002.

Stitchin, Zacharia. *The Stairway to Heaven*. New York: Avon Books, 1980.

Streiber, Whitley. *The Coming Global Superstorm*. New York: PocketStar Books, 1999.

Talbot. Michael. *The Holographic Universe*. Harper Perennial, 1991.

Tompkins, Peter. *Secrets of the Great Pyramid*, New York: Galad Books, 1971.

Von Ward, Paul. *Gods, Genes and Consciousness*. San Francisco: Hampton Roads, 2004,

Wright, Robert. *Non-Zero: The Logic of Human Destiny*. New York: Random House, 2000.

Photo Credits

All photographs used are in the public domain unless otherwise identified:

P. 14 courtesy of www.e-yakimono.net and www.japanesepottery. com; p. 15 sec 3 (a) and (b) courtesy of Philip Rychel; p. 18–19 Satellite image by GeoEye, courtesy of Googlemaps in compliance with terms of use: http://code.google.com/apis/maps/terms.html; p. 20 courtesy of Googlemaps in compliance with terms of use: http://code.google. com/apis/maps/terms.html; p. 24 crystalinks; p. 27 courtesy of the Library of Congress; p. 34 courtesy of Dr. Silvia Gonzalez, Liverpool's John Moores University–Bournemouth University; p. 45, courtesy of World-mysteries.com; p. 50 Josef F. Blumrich, Ezekiel's wheel, PD= http://www.bibliotecapleyades.net/sitchin/spaceships_ezekiel.htm; p. 64, photos used with permission of Dennis Balthaser; p.96 courtesy of University of Arlington Special Collection; p. 77 photo taken by Lynne D. Kitei, M.D. on 10/10/01, www.thephoenixlights.net, courtesy of Dr. Kitei. Phoenix lights, crop circle photos appearing on pp. 102, 109, 110, courtesy of Lucy Pringle.

ABOUT THE AUTHOR

Jerry Kroth, Ph.D. is an Associate Professor in the Graduate counseling psychology program at Santa Clara University. He teaches psychotherapy and personality theory, dreamwork, and research methods. He has an abiding therapeutic interest in working with dreams, personal oracles, and the applications of dream theory to psychohistory. Jerry has been a member of the International Psychohistorical Association since 1983.
Dr. Kroth's seven prior books were in the areas of counseling psychology, child sexual abuse, learning disorders, metapsychology, and research methodology. In addition he has written and presented over 75 papers on anxiety, child development, mass psychology, synchronicity, experimental studies of the dream process, the psychology of propaganda, psychohistory and collective psychology. He is also a contributor to the Huffington Post. His most recent book is *Conspiracy in Camelot: the complete history of the assassination of John Fitzgerald Kennedy* (New York: Algora, 2003). Professor Kroth lives in California with his wife and two daughters.

INDEX